John Oliver Hobbes

The Gods, some Mortals and Lord Wickenham

John Oliver Hobbes

The Gods, some Mortals and Lord Wickenham

ISBN/EAN: 9783743337152

Manufactured in Europe, USA, Canada, Australia, Japa

Cover: Foto ©ninafisch / pixelio.de

Manufactured and distributed by brebook publishing software (www.brebook.com)

John Oliver Hobbes

The Gods, some Mortals and Lord Wickenham

CONTENTS

CHAP.		PAGE
I.	AN ARISTOCRATIC HOUSEHOLD	1
II.	WHICH CONTAINS A BRIEF WELCOME, A LITTLE HISTORY, AND A LONG FAREWELL	9
III.	LORD WICKENHAM	24
IV.	IN WHICH WARRE DISPLAYS A FORGOTTEN TALENT	29
V.	AN EXCURSION INTO THE SORDID AND A FLIGHT INTO RHETORIC	43
VI.	A LITTLE LOVE, A LITTLE SCIENCE	67
VII.	A SOLILOQUY DURING THE SMALL HOURS	85
VIII.	CONTRITION IN THE ROBUST	92
IX.	MORTAL HAPPINESS	102
X.	A WEDDING	117
XI.	TWO MEN AND TWO WIVES	123

CHAP.		PAGE
XII.	DISILLUSION	132
XIII.	REALITY	161
XIV.	MORE REALITIES	168
XV.	PLAIN FACTS	188
XVI.	A PRELUDE	209
XVII.	THE UNLOVELY	213
XVIII.	WICKENHAM	221
XIX.	THE UNSPOKEN	234
XX.	IN WHICH WARRE REASONS WHILE ANNE READS	252
XXI.	IN WHICH THE AUTHOR SPEAKS	259
XXII.	ALLEGRA	262
XXIII.	ACCIDENTS AND THE INEVITABLE	270
XXIV.	AN EPISODE	276
XXV.	LORD WICKENHAM'S COMMUNICATION TO THE AUTHOR	278
XXVI.	THE LAST	288

The Gods, some Mortals and Lord Wickenham

CHAPTER I

An Aristocratic Household

A GUEST was expected at the Palazzo Vendramini. A large red man in a pale livery many sizes too small was lighting the one gas-lamp which hung over the entrance, and which only served to call vain shadows out of the barren gloom.

"Who goes there?" he cried suddenly.

"It is I, Antonio."

The young girl who came forward seemed to have been whipped up into a fragile existence from the very cream of tenderness, weakness, love, and folly. Her oval face, small, full lips, and mysterious black hair had the romance of other centuries than this—poetic inhumanity of a sonneteer's mistress. Although her figure was not too slight, it was lost in her loose-fitting black dress, made after the schoolroom pattern with a straight, full skirt, and a bodice pleated in empty folds. A châtelaine hung from her belt, and its silver chains chattered as she walked.

"The Signor is late, Contessina," said Antonio.

Allegra blushed, and pretended to be groping in her pocket. "I have lost my thimble," she said. "I did not think that the Signor was late. I am looking for my thimble."

The man picked up a broom which stood in the corner of his lodge, and with magnificent indolence began to sweep the floor. "If it is here this will find it," he said.

Allegra leant against the balustrade, and held her hands over her face—partly to protect it from the dust and partly to conceal her expression, which hovered between laughter and some secret anxiety.

"When there is a pilgrimage the trains are always late," said Antonio. "I wonder the Signor did not come a day sooner."

The girl drew a long breath. "Ah!" she exclaimed, "I had forgotten the pilgrimage. He may not be here for another hour. Why did I forget the pilgrimage?"

"They happen so often," grumbled the man;

"it is a cheap way of getting to Rome. No wonder there is so much piety!" He dropped the broom, stretched out his arms, and yawned. "The thimble is not here."

But Allegra had already disappeared, and was flying up the stairs like a bird through a cloud of smoke. Antonio could just hear the occasional flick of her skirts against the wall, and the jingle of her châtelaine. Presently a door closed, and all was silent. Antonio returned to his lodge and resumed that long siesta, his existence, which the duties of hall-portership so rudely and intemperately disturbed.

It was not all cakes and ale in the service of Tito, Count Vendramini, and Allegra, his daughter; breakfast was served late at the Palazzo, and dinner rarely. The Count was a gentleman of military renown, who, in his youth, had married a poor lady for love, but who now bought and sold objects of art on commission. The fortune he had amassed by this means, however, added more lustre to his integrity than clothes to his back; if not shabby, his raiment spoke of adventure, and, although he always appeared as a man of fashion, one felt that his tailor was not so indulgent as his valet was ingenious. Vendramini was to be met at the best houses; he had a charming, stupid manner, great fluency in light conversation, and none of that wit which creates enmity and renders friendship an inglorious combat. His eyes only directed their gaze on the finest feature of each face, his ears only caught the happiest remarks, his heart only thrilled at the noble motive in every action; in fact, he was by nature what most of us fail to become even by laborious art—an extremely agreeable person. The superb desolation of his Palazzo was the stately background of a career which one touch of cunning would have made contemptible, and which, if the actor had been less sincere, could so easily have seemed absurd. The great stone building had within its walls an empty picture-gallery, fountains which never played, a garden without plants, and a ball-room in which no beauty had danced for fifty years. Yet, in this tomb of a once princely dignity, the Count had but three desires: to prolong his own life to the utmost limit of human existence, to make one day a really good bargain, and to find his daughter a husband. He had been left a widower just at the age when a man stands in most need of a patient, admiring companion, and when the idea of a second marriage is charming to him in the same degree that his friends would think such an act on his part supremely foolish

Ridicule has a longer roll of martyrs than either love or religion, and poor Vendramini, being a man of ardent whims rather than strong passions, contented himself by wedding in imagination only all the eligible ladies of his acquaintance as they happened to pass under his notice. He admired them all, and saw himself in circumstances of extreme felicity with any one of them; each was his dear, and he was the dearest of each; they were ever faithful and he was ever courtly—few husbands own such fine regard, such esteem, such consideration, for the wives of their bosom as the Count entertained for these partners of his daily dreaming. But a visionary wife, with all her merits, graces, and variety, cannot give advice, and Vendramini wanted advice. Allegra was now seventeen; he only knew her as the one woman whom it had never occurred to him to marry. His paternal instinct taught him nothing further. He had been desperately fond of her mother, for she was pretty, and passionate, and provoking—a lady who had the gaiety of a light o' love and the modesty of a virgin saint—it was not in the nature of the man to tire of anything so artificial, so preposterous. He had first met her at Baden-Baden, where, as the natural daughter of Lord Denborough by the naughty

Duchess of A., she won the undisguised pity of every lady born in lawful wedlock, and the sly admiration of the men. She possessed great beauty, distinguished manners, and no money. It was very reasonably assumed that she would spend the best years of her life as a Peer's mistress, and in her repentant autumn marry a Colonel of Dragoons. When the Count Vendramini demanded her hand in marriage he took a candid pride in his own unworldliness, which, at one stroke, gave glory to God, annoyance to his friends, and an honourable name to the only woman on earth he felt unworthy of. But Allegra was unlike her English mother; her glance was cold, and she did not understand the subtleties of domestic virtue. The Count liked to sit in his library with his friend Cardinal Villard, and think how happy his daughter ought to be alone by herself in the next room. It was insupportable when they sat opposite each other, and, in the hope of conjuring up a home-like atmosphere, talked about the repairs which they were too poor to effect, the Pope's health, and salad-dressing. Allegra was no companion for a man who had such a repugnance for plain facts that he could only eat fruit when it was crystallised. The care of finding her a husband, however, was not one to make nights sleepless, or mornings over-long. The girl was pretty, and it was known that she had a rich godmother in England. Suitors smiled from all sides: some of them were well born, many very handsome, a few were not much poorer than the Count himself; he might easily have been bewildered by the difficulty of choosing an appropriate son-in-law out of the decorative and decorated mob which composed his Saturday receptions. Allegra, unhappily, had no eyes for these gentlemen; she disliked the Italian character, which was unsympathetic to her prim, even prudish mind. She had been taught the proprieties by an elderly woman who had been her mother's nurse, and whose life had been one undeviating observance of the genteel; who was Protestant in faith, and Scotch by birth, and who exhibited at once the most austere traits of her creed and her nation. This good, if formidable, creature had assured Allegra that there was but one man whom she could with any good manners marry, and this was her father's friend—Dr. Simon Warre, of Grosvenor Street, in London. Warre had spent a week at the Palazzo on several occasions, and was one of the Count's most constant customers. He was forming a private museum—an expensive hobby for a bachelor; it was a pity he had no better use for his guineas. Thus spake spinsterial wisdom. He was the visitor for whom Antonio was watching when he lit the lamp and Allegra came in search of her thimble

CHAPTER II

Which contains a Brief Welcome, a Little History, and a Long Farewell

AN hour passed. Vendramini grew impatient for Warre's arrival. There was a concert at the Quirinale that evening, and the social instinct no less than duty urged the Count's attendance at the Palace. He delayed his departure till the walls could no longer contain him, when, leaving Allegra to assure his guest that Court etiquette often made one impolite even to one's most cherished friends, he stepped into his rickety chariot and drove away.

When Warre was at last announced, Allegra was waiting alone in the Salon, a large, grim room, bare in spite of its green silk hangings, and dingy, with all its wealth of tarnished gilt. The girl sat on the pompous sofa, her strange little figure perched solitary and self-possessed in its environment of unrelieved and ghostly melancholy

—a melancholy made more funereal by the scattered wax-candles which burned as they do in a chamber of death, giving light without life, and flame without cheer. The man and the girl looked at each other with frank curiosity. They had not met for two years. Warre was tall, broad-shouldered, and, although not strictly handsome, his face had the heroic intention. His eyes were grey, and but for the richness of their colour would have been over-brilliant—coldly-bright; as it was, they formed a perplexing contrast to the rather sombre, even sullen expression of his other features. He heard Allegra's words of greeting, and her explanation of Vendramini's absence, but as things remote, unnecessary, and meaningless.

"How you have changed!" he said abruptly. The quick blush which tinted her whole face was comparable only to the effect of a little red wine poured into clear spring water. She made no reply, but led the way down a long corridor into the dining-room. Its ponderous oak door stood open; he could see the window beyond curtained with faded silk rep, the long table, the carved sideboard of English design, and the mirror on which two mahogany Cupids sat, for ever drawing aside a mahogany veil. Allegra sat facing him, and stitched at a piece of embroidery while he ate his supper, which was served by two men, one of whom was evidently new to the establishment, although his livery had an air of long and faithful service. There was very little attempt at conversation. Allegra was shy, and Warre was either so absorbed in his own thoughts, or so bewildered by the fatigue of his journey, that the silence seemed natural and pleasant. When he had finished his meal, she rose and wished him good-night.

"What!" said he; "must you go? I am only beginning to know you."

"I always go to bed at ten."

"Then you ought to have been there two hours ago. How good of you to sit up so late on my account."

"Papa wished it. I was very pleased to obey him. Good-night." She spoke English with delicious precision, giving each syllable a musical value; otherwise her accent did not betray her Italian birth. After she had gone, Warre remained in a long reverie, which was more lively than sleep, and yet less clear than waking. Hitherto he had always thought of Allegra as a pretty excuse for buying sweetmeats. How she had changed! Why had he come to Rome? Why had he brought—in spite of his man's remonstrances to the contrary—his dullest clothes and least youthful ties? Why had he forgotten that the spring air was warm? He had been working hard, and talking a great deal about matters which did not amuse him—or any one else—in the least; he felt stale, jaded, depressed, with only a vague notion that he would like to doze for a week or so and say nothing. The Vendramini found miracles of wit even in his yawns, and the Count was a dear fellow, a sweet old bore, who, after all, knew a great deal about the Etruscan remains. Small wonder that Rome should figure in Simon's mind as the city of repose and pleasant relaxation. How the little girl had changed!

A night's rest dimmed the unearthly romance of his first encounter with Allegra; he almost dreaded meeting her again, lest she should find that his interest had waned, and he discover that her enchantment fled before the sunrise. Man is ever miserly with his illusions; if to gain two he must risk one, he shrinks from the venture. Simon wanted to remember Allegra always as she had looked when he arrived. He took breakfast with Vendramini, and lent an intelligent ear to an account of the concert, a learned analysis of the sonatas which were played, and a minute description of the gown worn—the flirtation executed—by each lady present.

The morning passed in restful stupidity, but that day, and during the days which followed, he saw Allegra seldom. Men should be careful how they wish. Warre could not think that she intended to avoid him, for her manner was always winning, her smile invariably sweet, her eyes, when they met his, full of kindness and sympathy. These unobtrusive graces, though baffling and, to a certain extent, unsatisfactory, were not without their fascination to a man who, in the small leisure left him by his work, was looking out for a wife who coupled an aristocratic lineage with an humble spirit, and beauty with demureness. He himself came of a distinguished family on his mother's side, but she had married a man many degrees beneath her in the social scale, and the son of this inauspicious match had found it a bitter task to assert his right to that society which, whether rightly or wrongly known as the best, alone consorted with his tastes and instincts. Since his profession was the one of all others which demands a wife as the signpost of decorum, it was remarkable that Warre had so long remained a bachelor, and had yet won a reputation for prudence, and led a life of apparent contentment which his married rivals could not better—which most of them had only too much cause to envy. The unhappy home of his childhood and youth, where the sordid tragedy of a disastrous marriage had played itself out in genteel poverty, small humiliations, and peevish discontent, must have tired the poetic aspirations of a man even more resolute to find the delight rather than the misery of existence than Simon Warre. His mother gave the text of her long years of little suffering when she admitted over her husband's coffin that it had always sounded disrespectful when he called her by her Christian name. Warre heard the remark, and was at first only sensitive to the grim humour of the situation. The fine lady at least lived to tell the tale ; the boor was dead. Then he remembered his father's good-nature, his deep but never-satisfied craving for the kitchen and back-stairs, his sublime endurance of an eternal education in matters of etiquette, refinement, and the gentlemanly arts, his meekness under taunts, his patience under neglect, his silence under the fretful humours of a selfish woman who knew too well that once in her life, at any rate, she had made an enormous sacrifice. Simon loved his mother, pitied her, encouraged her arrogance. She possessed the one gift which, in his eyes, atoned for every shortcoming—great personal beauty ; yet as he stood by his father's grave, and heard the muttered prayers of an impatient curate, the discordant hymn wailed by mourners, who were not so despairing but they could shout themselves into resignation; when he saw the extravagant fears lest the widow should catch cold, and the frantic desire of the funeral guests to escape from the vulgar dust, whose glorious resurrection had been pronounced as sure and certain in a considerate undertone, he felt a fierce and choking shame for his mother's want of heart, which he had never known for the dead man's lack of breeding.

For a week after the burial Lady Henrietta Warre found much to congratulate herself in the fact that she received letters of condolence and even calls from most of the relatives with whom she had quarrelled at the time of her marriage. But when these had displayed their Christian feeling and gratified their curiosity at the fact of learning that she lived in lodgings at West Kensington, and would probably need assistance if she were once encouraged to dine out, they had the delicacy not to intrude further upon her sorrow, which, as they each and all insisted, would of course be life-long, irremediable, and only to be endured in an unbroken solitude. Like most women, Lady Henrietta learnt nothing from the mistakes, the disappointments, the revelations which each year brings. She had no philosophy, and her opinion of religion was so high that she would have considered it profane to apply its consolations to the ordinary troubles of a common day. She preferred instead to rail against the injustice, the selfishness, and the spite of every creature she had ever met or heard of, and to weep incessantly over her unmerited misfortunes.

Yet a worse affliction was in store for her. Simon entered himself as a student at the Imperial College Hospital. His paternal uncle—who had married a draper's shop but whose love was science—supplied the fees with plebeian generosity, and, in order to stimulate the youth's ambition, never failed to address him in the intimacy of the domestic circle as *Sir Simon Warre, Bart., G.C.B., M.D., F.R.S.* Lady Henrietta may not have been altogether insensible to this solace, although she often wailed her recollection of the time when a gentleman would no more dream of sitting down to dinner with his doctor than with his attorney or his bootmaker. She refused to acknowledge that her son was under any necessity to earn a penny: he would marry a rich wife, and then all his titled relatives would take interest in him. He could go into Parliament. In the meantime she promised to do all in her power to thwart *the medical idea*. The boy would often journey to and fro the hospital and West Kensington three or four times a day in obedience to her crazy notes on the subject of frozen waterpipes, insolent servants, acute headaches, heart seizures, alarming fits of depression, sudden fears for his own health, and the like. What a struggle it was! What an effort to keep pace with the other students! What a sickening fight against time, fatigue, and failure! When he attempted to work in the evening, his mother would either flounce out of the room, threatening suicide as the one amusement left her, or sit opposite to him alternately sulking, whimpering, and scolding.

"Why don't you talk?" she would say. "You take no interest in me. I wish I were dead. You think of nothing but those disgusting books. I never knew any one so selfish. You never offer to read aloud to me, and you know how I delight in Pusey's Sermons! I have devoted my life to you, made every sacrifice for you, and—I am not very strong!" Here she would moan in self-pity, protesting that no one loved her, that there was no place in the world for an affectionate, loyal, and devoted woman, that Simon was his father's son—coarse-minded, brutal, incapable of understanding a lady's disposition. The lad endured this martyrdom for three years, at the end of which time his health broke down; nor did he give any hope of recovery till one fine day a rumour reached him that, should he live, it was Lady Henrietta's intention to signify her gratitude to the Almighty by marrying the vicar of their parish. A month later he was able to support her ladyship through the wedding ceremony, and if there was any creature in London happier than the bridegroom it was Simon when he kissed the bride good-bye. She was his mother, and he loved her, but he felt he could never again pass under the terrible scourge of her authority. He must be his own master.

He shared lodgings with a fellow-student near the hospital, rose at five in the morning, worked till eleven o'clock at night, talked to the patients for recreation, and earned the money for his rent by writing humorous articles on art, politics, and literature for a Society journal. Four times a week, too, he attended classical lectures at the Imperial College, where a distinguished scholar hurled instruction at a scribbling crowd of youths and eager women, who appeared to write with their noses and hear with their heels, and who regarded the Pagan philosophers, poets, and wits as terriers do rats. Nor were lighter distractions wanting. Since Simon was a fine-looking fellow, with courtly manners, the doctors' wives received him gladly, invited him to their less formal tea-parties, treated him—to all outward showing—as their social equal. One of them even formed the project of marrying him to her plainest daughter; but whether he did not suspect her condescension, or whether, knowing it, he was too modest to accept so portentous an honour, the plan miscarried.

Before he obtained his degree he won a Travelling Scholarship, went abroad, and returned two years later, mysterious, silent, curiously unwilling to offer any opinion even on his own right to exist. They feared he would come to nothing; he was, therefore, chosen as the fittest man for an assistant-lectureship then vacant. The post was cheerfully offered, meekly accepted. The Senior Pathologist suffered himself to doze, sure that he would not be missed, sure that no inconvenient genius had arisen to make him reconsider the highly excellent old lectures which he had chanted for twelve years, and without the humiliating fatigue of a second thought. But he sauntered into the class-room one afternoon to find it overcrowded, and Warre demonstrating heresy with an eloquence as convincing as it was unprofessional. The two exchanged glances, and at once comprehended each other to that pitch of cock-sureness which is known as a misunderstanding. A few days later Simon sent in his resignation; the

Dean expressed his regret and looked his relief; murmured well-known maxims about things in general, and, with official tenderness, advised him *to be careful.*

In the following year Warre, then five-and-twenty, got his degree, and, under the inspiration of an occasional square meal, wrote an Essay which gained him a prize and an appointment at the Knightsbridge Hospital. From that day his success was steady, his ability acknowledged; he had many critics but few enemies, a large and amiable acquaintance, some two or three staunch friends, and a baker's dozen of aristocratic relatives who, having ignored him as a student, now found it amusing to talk of " that clever, eccentric cousin of ours who went in for science, and who is the coming man on Paralysis." At seven-and-twenty, with good health, good intentions, a good reputation, and an increasing income, one is not disposed to be misanthropic. Warre enjoyed his life; he thought it an altogether splendid thing to be alive; talked with confidence about the survival of the fittest, and declared his own willingness to surrender when a mightier than he should enter the field. Happiness, he assured his aged patients, was far more common than was generally supposed. No creature was undeservedly wretched if one tested his grievance by the light of reason and the laws of nature. It was inspiring to hear him. True, his rosy-toed philosophy had not been forced to trip over the red-hot ploughshares of pain and its attendant devils ; but he knew what it meant to be hungry, to be cold, to be sick at heart and wild in brain. All that, however, was of his own choosing ; he need not have worked, he might have stayed quietly at home with his mother at West Kensington, drinking tea, fondling the cat, and escorting lady-callers to the omnibus. " Each man has two fates," he would say ; " one is a free gift, the other is a prize, but the prize must be striven for." An intelligent youth this ; wisely dispassionate, on the best of terms with the Almighty, roaring lions, and the rest, fearing no man. The world, quick to appreciate audacity, spoke with confidence of his future. He would arrive ; but where ?

Warre remained in Rome ten days, and he woke the last morning to remember that he must return to that well-furnished emptiness in Grosvenor Street he called his home. He would miss Allegra. Adorable child ! Fairy, angel, poem, picture, melody—everything seductive, alluring, and inspiring except —a woman. He could, it is true, imagine her as a kind of immaterial wife—a sweet, feminine spirit as subtle as a sunbeam, but, alas ! as intangible. Yet when he had not seen her for some hours, and the remembrance of her forbidding innocence was not too vivid, he would be startled to find how ardently he desired her companionship—her presence—how oppressive the air seemed when she was not near; how the mere sound of her footstep made his heart cease beating; how he lost himself when he sought to read her eyes. All this distressed him; he had rested, and was in the mood for exalted sentiments, for love-making, for marriage, but Allegra was a little girl . . . a little girl. He had passed through a few romantic adventures: had loved, resisted, and regretted; had loved, not resisted, and regretted also; he had no overmastering belief in the permanency, the seriousness of any passionate attachment between men and women. He could not, therefore, bring himself to do more than own that if Allegra had been older, and had betrayed any strong regard for him, he would have asked her to become his wife, would have loved her better than discretion might permit him to express. But the glance, the word, the movement which would have fired this affection was not given. On the day of his departure, Allegra was even more silent, more anxious to escape from sight, than on the evening when he arrived. She had at least blushed over her welcome, but when he said good-bye her face was pale and inexpressive; she murmured a hope that he would have a pleasant journey, and brushed a stray thread from her sleeve.

The Count, who drove with Warre to the station, talked on the way of the solitariness of life, the sorrow of partings. He grew sentimental on the subject of his own forlorn state, and the difficulty he experienced in understanding Allegra. " She is so reserved, so timid," he said ; " it is impossible to tell what is passing in her mind. Yet what sum is too large to settle on a wife who can adore without asking questions? Most women are so inquisitive. They mistake curiosity for devotion to our interests. Poor Allegra! Although she is silent I think she suffers great tragedies !"

Warre marvelled that any man could be so mistaken in his own flesh and blood. O Science! art thou not also sometimes in error?

CHAPTER III

Lord Wickenham

THE fancies Warre had allowed himself to indulge in, under the spell of Rome, idleness, and a pair of dark eyes, vanished when he reached London. One glance at the Grosvenor Street house was enough to convince him that it and Allegra belonged to different worlds. The gloom of the Palazzo Vendramini was sublime; but this neat grey dwelling, which rested on the universe with the stubborn serenity of a visiting-card on a hall-table, had a dulness worse than human. Each window, too, looked like a patient eye watching for the careful housewife who should be there, and was not. As Warre crossed the threshold his spirits sank. Home-returning is a dreary performance when there is no devoted, if silly, woman to bask in one's dusty smiles. Simon thanked God that he was dining out that evening with his friend Wickenham.

Lord Wickenham was the only son of a saint, by

a fool. The saint died young, and the fool married another husband, who was considered, perhaps with justice, a greater dolt even than herself. Since it will not be necessary to refer to either of them again, it may be added that these beings lived to an advanced age, and finally departed this world, leaving no history, but two extremely neat epitaphs —one to the effect that we are not dead until we are forgotten, and the other advertising the peaceful end of one who was twice a widow. Lord Wickenham had been educated at Harrow and at Christ Church, Oxford, had made the Grand Tour, had planted trees, had observed the traditions of his house with correctness and good taste. The Wickenhams had a horror of precocity: no Wickenham had ever won a prize either at school or university; no Wickenham had ever distinguished himself before the age of forty-five; no Wickenham but had been thought a dunce for three-fourths of his career; and no Wickenham but had somehow contrived to die, like Mirabeau, leaving the world to wonder what on earth he could *not* have accomplished if he had only lived a day longer. Wickenham was now thirty, and, to the alarm of his relatives, betrayed, in unregarded moments, an interest in politics and an ability in discussing them not unworthy of Palmerston at his worst.

A rumour was also abroad that he was taking lessons in bricklaying, vine-culture, flute-playing, and astronomy. Had he any idea of founding a new Empire? The family took counsel with Warre; expressed a desire to read something concise on paralysis of the brain; bethought themselves of a Wickenham (described in Burke as "a learned man"), who, in the thirteenth century, had killed himself untimely, writing twelve thousand villainous verses, all in Latin, on six hundred different subjects. Two such in the race would point to hereditary disease—a taint of pedagogy. O Heavens! Save our Wickenham!

The process of salvation was now in full swing. Wickenham and Warre had journeyed together round lakes and through cathedrals; had climbed up the Alps; had suffered each other's sprained ankles and faced each other's skinned noses; knew each other's taste in food; had exchanged views on female beauty; were agreed that a fellow should marry the woman of his affections—when possible; each knew that there were events in the other's career which, though they would have no place in his biography (to be published in three volumes, and dedicated to a truth-loving nation), had made imperishable marks on his character; they were comrades.

"Thank God, I have got Wickenham," thought Warre once more, as he drove up to his friend's town-house in Gifford Street, Piccadilly. His next ejaculation was less pious, for, to his chagrin, he observed a brougham already at the door, and a lady and gentleman alighting therefrom. He knew them—Wickenham's country cousins—the Mereford Maukin-Fawkeses, Mr. and Mrs., both dull, one rich, one mournful.

"Is he going to give a party?" groaned Warre. Lo! two hansoms now blocked the way. Warre's coachman is in the wrong; must turn. The triumphant cabmen, with rattling of glass windows and banging of doors, deliver, first a man and next two ladies. One lady has a foot disproportionately small to scientific eyes—pretty, nevertheless. Impossible to see her face. But her petticoat, snow-white, has a row of little tucks near the hem. What hours must have been spent in stitching them! The vanity of women! At this point Simon remembered, with a sigh of regret, that few men were fit to be seen after two nights spent in the sleepless luxury of a sleeping-car. It was unfair on Wickenham's part not to have reminded him that there would be high heels to entertain at dinner. And who was the fellow in the first hansom? He had long hair and a little nose;

was, no doubt, a wit. Warre was in that gay and adventurous mood which the skippers of old must have had, when, the sea being too calm, they would whistle for the wind. His soul had, for the moment, become a mere grin : he was an incarnate Titter.

Lord Wickenham's residence presented an unpretentious exterior. While its architecture admitted of a portico and a balcony, the one was so small that it looked like the entrance to a birdcage, and the other was too narrow to stand upon. Although Warre knew the house as well as his own, he always felt a thrill of surprise and delight when the squat door was opened and he could step into the hall. Here another world disclosed itself—grand, splendid, and majestic, created when life, no less than art, was long, and crafts had not rotted into trades. Simon went up the wide marble staircase, the walls of which were hung with old Flemish tapestry representing the Triumph of Love over Worldliness, the Conflict between Youth and the Seven Deadly Sins, and similar allegorical subjects. Having crossed an ante-chamber, famous for its miniatures, and the great library, he found his host in a small room furnished in tulipwood and rose-velvet, which was consecrated to Gainsborough's painting of the supremely beautiful " Eliza, Lady Wickenham."

CHAPTER IV

In which Warre displays a Forgotten Talent

FROM Dr. Simon Warre to the Count Vendramini

"MY DEAR VENDRAMINI,—

"I have just returned from dining with Wickenham; dear Wickenham; incorruptible Wickenham of the square jaw; six-foot-three in his stockings; divine lunatic; luminous imbecile. What man in Europe can, with so little premeditation, utter so much good sense? Have you ever met him? To-night he gave a dinner-party —the Duchess of Wark, Mrs. Algernon Dane, the Maukin-Fawkeses, Stanley Breakspeare, Lawrence Tarraway, and a mysterious Miss Passer, whom Emma Wark eyed with some severity. Miss Passer was tall, with superb shoulders and a swelling throat; wearing no jewels nor meekest ornament, she had the sunny air of those primeval simpletons who were naked but not ashamed.

Her radiant eyes showed the delicious void and glorious colour of that blue sky we see in Italy; the calm of Heaven, without its unnatural holiness, dwelt in her gaze. Brown lashes, long and lustrous, shadowed this splendour, and hair, honestly golden, sparkling with sincerity, framed a face of such inexcusable loveliness that to behold it filled one with a suspicion of the Creator's benevolence. As I have said, Emma Wark, most romantic of discreet matrons, homeliest of worldlings, best of good souls, observed Miss Passer, and was troubled. Wickie, her friend, Warre, her cousin, and this terribly gifted young person. She saw it all! There would be the devil to pay. I already had that ecstatic absence of mind which is the earliest symptom of a mortal enamoured. Wickie, more inscrutable because so apparently transparent, seemed much as usual. (In any case, Wickenham in love is only Wickenham over-sober; the sobriety of his passions must puzzle even the Recording Angel. Are they passions at all?)

"Conversation buzzed with drooping wings and feeble drone through our little group, so lamentable is the effect of one beautiful stranger among devoted friends. Miss Passer and Mrs. Maukin-Fawkes discussed in dying tones the huge benefit they had derived from sea-air. Stanley Breakspeare and Mrs. Algernon Dane could not decide how many months had elapsed since their last meeting; each felt that it did not matter in the smallest degree one way or the other, and neither took the trouble to look concerned. Maukin-Fawkes confided to the Duchess that his brute of a doctor had forbidden him all food except charcoal biscuits; he no longer enjoyed dining out; thought seriously of going to Norway—to shoot elk. Or was he thinking of some other beastly place? His memory—under charcoal—had suffered. If he wasn't better in a fortnight he would change his medical adviser. Dundy of Brook Street gave everybody dry champagne and raw eggs. If eggs did not suit you, you could use your own judgment. But then, one does not pay a fellow two guineas to be told to use your own judgment! What an insult to one's intelligence! After all, there was something to be said for charcoal; the best science nowadays was always opposed to common sense. 'I have a taste for science,' he added modestly. Emma Wark assumed the nice consternation which all well-bred persons display when their friends own to any talent. 'Can it be possible?' she looked; 'do I hear aright? Have *you* a taste for science? Who would have guessed it?"

"The progress of the guests to the dining-room was the quick work of a long minute. I was seated at the table before I realised that Miss Passer's hand had, for a second, rested butterfly-like on my own, and had, as delicately, been withdrawn. Her first act was a careful study of the menu: she puckered her divine brows, and, at intervals, seemed to be searching her memory for the precise flavour of some particular dish. Once her expression said clearly, 'Do I really like quails? When did I eat them last, and where?' She made no attempt at conversation till we reached the fourth course. I thought her greediness quite charming; it was so natural, so human, so unconscious, yet perfectly graceful. She ate slowly, lingering over each morsel; there was no hint of voracity in her appetite. It refreshed a student of Paralysis to see such health. I did my utmost to amuse this exquisite example of a sane body, female of sex, angelic in appearance. Occasionally she smiled at my wit, showing thereby a sufficiently good, nay, rather an amazing intelligence! Having reached roast saddle of mutton, she owned to a tenderness for all that was beautiful in life. She had a pet bird that was ungrateful, that had once bitten her finger—see, the scar!—but she had not the courage to scold it, to even show anger. The bird was so pretty. Extraordinary sympathy in tastes, in morals, in point of view! If I, too, had owned such a bird, and it had bitten me even to the heart, I would have forgiven it all, and died, worshipping its beauty. Was that weak?

"'Manly,' murmured Miss Passer; 'heroic!'

"'Oh no,' said I, 'not heroic.'

"'*I* think so.' Here followed a discussion on what was, properly speaking, heroism, and what a mere matter of instinct. It was a man's instinct to adore the admirable—to desire it eagerly—in whatever guise it might appear. She supposed this was indeed the case, and sighed. Melancholy became her. She wore it with celestial resignation. No peevishness marred the serenity of that May-morning countenance. How young she was! I asked whether this was her first season.

"She replied that she was in the musical profession; had sung several times in public; was to sing at the Rothschilds' this coming week. Mrs. Dane had been extremely kind to her, and had given her many introductions. Singing was hard work, but a voice was her only gift.

"'Sensible woman,' said I; 'you have no desire to adapt souls for Paradise. You do not try to make virgins out of mud and conquerors out of sawdust.' (I have no notion what this means, but it sounded rather well when I said it.) She owned that she was not at all clever, and did not understand social questions. She only wished that spotted veils would go out of fashion. They hurt her eyes. I was not slow to accept this invitation to look into them, nor did I pretend that my interest was purely scientific; indeed, I should have been annoyed if she had thought so. We continued our fooling. Mrs. Maukin-Fawkes to the left, and Lawrence Tarraway to the right, suffered neglect, and by no means in the Christian spirit. They coughed manners, looked morality, and drummed with their fingers the funeral march of my future.

"'Simon seems very happy,' said Emma Wark to Wickenham. (He repeated the conversation to me later.)

"' And why not?' asked Wickie.

"The question was not to be answered at random. 'If it were suitable,' she observed, after an unuttered but violent argument conveyed to her opponent in a series of smothered sighs, curls of the nostril, and swift, needle-sharp glances in the direction of Miss Passer—' If it were suitable,' she repeated, 'I should be the first to rejoice. But it looks disastrous.'

"'Why?' said Wickenham.

"'Busy men should not marry pretty wives,' said Emma. 'And ... who is she?'

"'A friend of Mrs. Dane's.'

"'Are they related to each other?'

"'I believe not.'

"'I hate mysteries,' said the lady, tossing her head.

"'If I could tell you anything more about her I would. Aren't you my conscience?'

"'No, or you would show more discretion,' was her tart reply.

"With all his amiability, Wickenham is not a man to brook the dictation of any Emma Wark. He is master of his own dinner-table, and for dinner-table read opinions, prejudices, sentiments, likes and dislikes. His independence of mind is extraordinary; his indifference to criticism shows a hardness of heart, a spirit of flint, not to be so much as named in his genial presence. It is not cold blood which flows in his veins, but *iced wine*.

"'My house is not a marriage-market,' he said, with a dignity peculiar to the noble family of Wickenham. 'I do not invite my friends to smile at each other here, because I want to groan at their wedding a little later!'

"Yet Emma, too, has spirit. 'My dear Wick,' she said; 'the genius of hospitality consists not so much in making people meet, but in helping them to *part*—on good terms. Remember that!' Wickenham never despises a good idea—even when offered by a woman. He told me he was greatly pleased with that remark, and made a note of it.

"After the ladies had left the table, discussion dropped the brisk air it had worn under their balmy influence, and we relapsed into silent meditation, liberally punctuated by full stops. Wickie is not a great talker, and is not the prince of listeners; he enjoys nothing so much as a long pause. For this reason geniuses are always ready to dine with him. They can leave their brilliancy at home, and bring their wives. At most houses the order is reversed. But this evening I was the nearest thing to genius present.

"Harold Maukin-Fawkes, M.P., is a man of gloomy disposition, who, nevertheless, takes it as a personal affront if any one about him ventures to display the least dulness. His melancholy needs gales of laughter to keep it fresh, otherwise it fades into mere jaundice. Stanley Breakspeare is a gossip, but he has an irritating habit of withholding his scandalous chronicle until every other man at the table has told the right stories about the wrong people. Sir Lawrence Tarraway, on the other hand, was born a really charming fellow, but he was once painted by Stanton Marlow, R.A., as 'Lucius Cornelius Sulla,' and his one hope now is to be mistaken for that immortal canvas. His life is rounded by a gilt frame; humanity does not touch him. Wickenham lives in the firm conviction that the picture will one day be destroyed by fire, and then Tarraway will be himself again.

"Maukin-Fawkes, perhaps because he was the only married man at the table, was the first to refer to Miss Passer as a devilish pretty woman, and to inquire whether she was an heiress. If not, why had Sarah Dane taken her up?

"'To tell the truth,' said Wickenham, 'I have not given the matter a moment's thought. Mrs. Dane asked me if she might bring her here to-night, and I said I should be delighted. I understand she has a beautiful voice.'

"'Amateur, I suppose?' said Maukin-Fawkes.

"'No. Mrs. Dane was careful to say that she was in the profession; that she wished to earn her own living. Plucky!'

"Maukin-Fawkes showed the horror which only a gentleman who had married for money could feel for any base dependent on a merely natural talent.

"'Mrs. Dane told me all about her,' said Stanley

Breakspeare, in a thrilling voice. 'She is the daughter of Sir Hugh Delaware. But he is in the Bank of England, and is as poor as a rat. He has been obliged to drop out of everything—even his club. Oddly enough, I saw the old cock when I popped into the Securities Office the other day about some beastly dividends. I opened the wrong door, and, instead of walking into the Manager's room, I found myself among the God-forgotten clerks. Ha! ha! You should have seen me bolt. But I noticed this old fellow at once. Ancient style, you know. Looks like Sir Robert Peel, and the Duke of Wellington, and those chaps—high collar, clean-shaven, hair sticking out above his ears. "Who's that swell?" I asked the Manager. "He would make his fortune playing earls and footmen in high comedy." "Sir," said he, "that gentleman is Sir Hugh Delaware, and one ot our most conscientious clerks." "Good God!" said I. "Poor devil!" I never heard anything so pathetic in my life. Take my oath! If you could have seen that magnificent old aristocrat, and heard that rotten little Cockney Manager calling him a conscientious clerk, as though he had some idea of giving him a tip at Christmas!' He swallowed some claret, and the rim of the wineglass made a sort of a ripple on the humane expression which the recital of this anecdote had called up on his countenance. 'Lady Delaware was a Pavenham,' he added at length.

"Maukin-Fawkes, who was now breathing more freely, made an observation. 'But the Pavenhams, too, are poor.'

"'Poor! I should think so,' said Breakspeare. 'I have heard that they have got even a skin less than most people.'

"'Why is the girl called Passer?' asked Maukin-Fawkes.

"'A *nom de guerre.*'

"'I wonder whether she makes much money, singing. She dresses well—far better than my wife!'

"Though Wickenham is by no means blind to the necessity of dowries, he abhors any open discussion of a woman's fortune; it seems to him like hall-marking the stars; his chivalry is discreet, but never commercial. He has a deep contempt for his cousin Maukin-Fawkes, who, for ten thousand a year, married a few pounds of chaste bone wrapped in lean flesh. Good Lord! While man's nature bears the taint of original sin it is impossible to love a woman so innocent of witchery as poor Ada Maukin-Fawkes. And marriage without some sort of sentiment is, say what you will, a revolting bargain. Wickie and I have never faltered in our agreement on this point.

"It is significant of our sympathy that at the same moment and in obedience to the same impulse we each made a remark which at once diverted curiosity from the subject of Miss Passer's possible income. Although the talk fell into the usual tittle-tattle about absent friends and acquaintances, Miss Passer's name did not occur again.

"In the next room, things, as I heard from Mrs. Maukin-Fawkes, were more formal. The Duchess of Wark is not ill-natured, but she has three unmarried sisters, and she probably could not see why Sarah Dane (who is, after all, a Carrigrohane, and who has some idea of *noblesse oblige*), she could not see why Sarah Dane should go out of her way to introduce a fascinating God-knows-who into their already over-womaned circle. Did it not smack of treachery? Her Grace has her own method of dealing with such satin foes. She turned her back on Mrs. Algernon Dane, and asked Miss Passer questions which, had that young creature been an impostor, must have riddled her soul. But Miss Passer, whose Christian name was Anne, only repeated the same simple tale she had confided to me at dinner. She was a singer, her voice was soprano. She had no intention of appearing in opera. Her people objected to the stage. It was extremely unlikely that the Duchess should have met either her father or her mother. They lived in great retirement in a tiny square near the Uxbridge Road. Passer was her professional name. The rest was mere smiling; she said no more. Poor Emma began to feel thoroughly ill at ease. No one could see Miss Anne Passer and not suspect that she was unnecessarily well born; she did not sit in that select circle like one who had rashly strayed into the wrong Paradise. If the Duchess could but have caught a hint of Delaware or Pavenham she would have clasped the newcomer to her bosom—figuratively, at all events. For she is staunch to her order . . . loyal to blood —whether its earthly tabernacle is situated near the Uxbridge Road or in East Hackney. But a Passer, suspiciously good-looking, who sang for her supper and perhaps danced for her lodging! Hence, upstart!

"When we joined them, Mrs. Algernon Dane at once wished Wickenham good-night, explaining that she had promised to take Anne to Lady Windegrave's party.

"'I am going to sing there,' added Miss Passer. The little speech was effective, and showed that she was not ashamed of her calling. After she had gone, no one had the courage to refer to her again.

"Good Heavens! What a long letter! I have not been so communicative since I wrote descriptive articles at half-a-guinea a column. Ah! those were the years of occasional dinners and daily eloquence. Now my dinners are daily and my eloquence only occasional. Remember me to Allegra, for I feel sure that she has already forgotten me.

"Yours,
"S. W."

In reading over this frankly artificial burst of confidence, which had been composed rather as a relief to his own feelings than for the Count's entertainment, Warre had sufficient self-knowledge to wonder whether he would have addressed it to Vendramini if there had not been an Allegra to be astonished at its contents. He hoped she would see how greatly he had admired the charming Anne Passer, and fell asleep thinking of a little girl, aged seventeen, in Rome.

CHAPTER V

An Excursion into the Sordid and a Flight into Rhetoric

WARRE awoke the next day with a firm determination to coax more enjoyment out of life, and, while he dressed, he sang with some gaiety :—

"Lovely Thaïs sits beside thee,
   Take the good the gods provide thee."

A week later he received a little note, bearing the Delaware crest, and signed with an "Anne Passer" which covered half the page. It ran thus :—

"18, SOUTHWICK TERRACE,
"HOLLAND PARK.

"DEAR DR. WARRE,—

"As you expressed so great an interest in modern Italian Music, it might amuse you—if you could spare the time—to call on Wednesday afternoon about five, when Signor Casmagni is coming to play us the first act of his new opera. The Danes have promised to come also.

"Yours sincerely,
"ANNE PASSER."

"No genius, this," he said to himself, and accepted the invitation in his wittiest manner.

Some time had passed since Warre had found occasion to drive into the densely populated deserts of Notting Hill and the Addison Road. In gazing at them once more, he had the sentiments of one revisiting a land of former exile: no released captive could have felt a more ardent melancholy at the sight of his prison-house than Simon experienced as he drove past the staring villas, hump-backed mansions, one-horned crescents, and crooked squares which give so deformed an aspect to that region which lies to the west of Hyde Park. He remembered his squalid lodgings in Bloomsbury with loyal affection, for the treasures in the British Museum give dignity to the meanest room, the poorest habitation, within its shade. There the atmosphere was heroic, scholarly, artistic; there, a man could feel himself the heir of all the ages in spite of an empty stomach and a pinched heart. Ah, he thought, poverty never kills the soul. The arch-destroyer is dull indolence, which under the name of Christian contentment, is but a slatternly acceptance of this world's dust and ashes. These and similar reflections went through the young doctor's head as he approached Southwick Terrace. No. 18 was a corner house, the front windows of which were draped with brown damask and white cotton lace—the former faded by the sun, the latter soiled and limp. Although summer's dust and winter's fog had formed a kind of moss over the brickwork, an air of disreputable animation distinguished the building from the forlorn and, to all outward showing, tenantless residences which made up the rest of the street. The paint on the door had worn away in some places and been scraped away in others by impatient feet and errant latchkeys; the bell hung wearily by a bent wire from its rusty socket; the steps showed the traces of many and strange boots. Warre's summons was answered, after a prolonged discussion in the area between male and female voices, by a Swiss man-servant, whose stained coat and insolent stare confirmed Simon's suspicion that the unfortunate Delawares were boarding with the cheerful family of some bankrupt speculator.

When he reached the drawing-room, a cuckoo clock struck the half hour, and as he had arrived rather earlier than he was expected, Anne was not there. A gentleman, whom he at once knew to be Sir Hugh Delaware, was sitting by the window with a little box of old feathers and odd ribbons by his side, making artificial flies. The Baronet was one of those men of gigantic stature and strength who are so fearful of exerting their superior force in some unfair or tyrannous way that they do not use it at all, and, from a false idea of generosity, suffer themselves to be ruled by beings and circumstances which the average pygmy would feel a coward in submitting to. His fine, serene countenance had the smoothness of marble, and, although he rarely smiled so vigorously as to disturb the lines of his mouth, there was an amiable tranquillity in his expression which presented all the effect of a perpetual simper. Whatever his thoughts may have been, he was not troubled by ideas, and the intelligence he displayed in the discharge of his duties at the Bank of England was that of a learned poodle, who, having been taught certain tricks, performs them he knows not why nor to what end. In the early part of his career he had spent his small fortune in riotous excess, driven fast horses, and been driven by a fast lady. This person, whom he could never be induced to abuse, was known as his "Ruin;" and

Lady Delaware, whom he had never been heard to praise, was called his "Salvation."

As Warre entered, Sir Hugh raised his eyes, and showed at a glance that he guessed who the visitor was. He rose, introduced himself, and sat down again.

"Pray do not let me interrupt your work," said Warre.

"I am very glad of an excuse to rest," said Delaware, with a languorous air of fatigue. "I have only three weeks' leave in the year," he went on, "and I spend the whole time angling at Wensley. I sold the place long ago to Ventry Coxe, but he is very civil—very civil, indeed, and lets me fish in the lake. We take lodgings in the town, and I enjoy the walk to the Manor. It is not more than five miles."

In making this unexpected reference to the sale of his family estate which had occurred some twenty years before under strangely disastrous conditions, Delaware showed neither regret nor sentiment, but had even something of the pride with which a veteran refers to the loss of a limb in battle. Whatever recollections it evoked, he fell into an unmeditative silence, surveying the room in which they sat with a tolerance verging on affection. The furniture was dingy and uncomfortable, consisting mainly of small bamboo tables, overburdened with vulgar ornaments, and chintz-covered chairs. Vases of discoloured and dyed Pampas grass, a gilt clock, and a pair of lustres adorned the mantelpiece; a few faded photographs of gentlemen in officers' uniform, ladies in dinner-dress, and babies in christening robes, stood on the cottage piano—a dolorous instrument with walnut legs and a green silk back. Two china lamps with yellow paper shades, resembling the tulle petticoats of a ballet-dancer, were placed on ebony stands in front of a long mirror framed in gilt carving made to represent pine-apples, fern leaves, and birds of paradise, a decoration which had no doubt been bought for a song, inasmuch as the glass was imperfect, and reflected all things not only hideously distorted, but through a mist.

The stillness was irresistible. Simon could find nothing to say, and found himself, like Sir Hugh, staring at the picture of pond-lilies, storks, and blue clouds which was painted in instalments on the door panels.

"I wonder," said Sir Hugh, at last, "whether the man has told my wife that you are here."

At that moment Lady Delaware came into the room. After Warre had been introduced, she showed her teeth in a perfectly kind manner, and explained that her daughter had been detained at a singing lesson; she would be with them in a few moments. The young man studied Anne Passer's mother with no ordinary interest. She looked like one of those trained canaries which are to be seen at country fairs, and which, dressed up in petticoats, give a pathetic imitation of human grace and dignity. Her expression was pensive; her figure, elegantly listless; the bonnet she wore was slightly awry, and her lace mantle seemed slipping from her shoulders. When she used her small, sad eyes of tearful tint it was only to fix them on her own hands, her own shoes, or on some object of her own attire. Warre felt that if—as her absent air implied—she had lost interest in the world, and her fellow-creatures, it was only because she had found the needs of Lady Delaware so much more profitable a study. She had married Sir Hugh because he was handsome, and because she would have died of jealousy if any other woman had captured him; but, with the morality peculiar to her sex, she had given society to understand, and never allowed him to forget, that in becoming his wife she was a martyr, and that in gratifying her own desires she had accepted a heavenly mission. For twenty sinners who can bear repentance, there is not one just person who can support the knowledge of having stirred a fellow-creature to remorse. Lady Delaware made it the amusement of her life to lead her husband out of temptation, and deliver him from evil, and, in helping the penitent to resist his tastes, she found many opportunities for the indulgence of her own. The cares of housekeeping on a small scale had proved too much for her temper. All the Pavenhams were more skilful in eating a cheap dinner than in ordering one. She had tried lodgings; she had attempted to control a furnished flat; she had shared a villa with a friend; and, as a last resort, had now adopted what she called the Continental plan of living *en pension*. Sir Hugh had followed her progression from one boarding-house to another, at first with reluctance, and at last with a real appetite for adventure. The constant change of scene gave a variety to his life which it would otherwise have lacked, and, as he was by nature philanthropic, he enjoyed dining at a long table with a number of persons, who, if they were not his dependents, looked as though they might have been.

No. 18, Southwick Terrace, was not more barren of luxury than most establishments of its class, and was considered sufficiently respectable by those whose only prejudices were directed against sinners who lacked discretion. The proprietress, who was an army surgeon's widow, called it a private hotel, and dined in her own apartment, usually in company with military—and other— cousins. From the social point of view, the Delawares were her most distinguished patrons; the rest had mysteriously fine names of the Greville-Stubbs and D'Eresby-Brown order, or professional dignities of obscure significance. The women minced and the men swaggered; a false decorum and a falser ease made the moral atmosphere a perpetual hurricane; jealousies, bickerings, and backbiting were like a plague of insects in the air. The life of the house would have been contemptible if, in regarding it, it had been possible to forget that each creature who took part in the struggle had an immortal soul. Lady Delaware bore her surroundings with an indifference which lookers-on might have taken for arrogance, good-nature, or stoic wisdom, but which in reality arose from a want of understanding. The only things which offended her taste at Southwick Terrace were the shabbiness of the furniture, the cotton sheets, the Swiss manservant, and the miserable soups. But gossip amused her; an exhibition of the pettiest emotion could always attract her curiosity, and, so long as that entertaining faculty could be engrossed, her patience never wavered. Hers was an inquisitiveness, too, which was as far removed from sympathy as old straw is from new-mown hay. If a friend broke his leg she would ask *in how many places, and whether he groaned*, and there her concern would end. She had heard from Anne that Dr. Warre was considered the coming man in his profession, that he was a bachelor, that she had met him at Lord Wickenham's. Before coming into the drawing-room, her ladyship had observed his brougham and its fine pair of roans standing at the front door, and these had greatly assisted her belief in his genius. It was characteristic of the woman that it did not enter her head to regard him as a possible son-in-law. Her one and only thought was a sense of thanksgiving to Providence that she had at last found a doctor of first-rate ability whom she could consult with regard to her own health, as often as necessary and without paying a fee.

The conversation of Lady Delaware was dry, formal, and a little condescending, uttered, too, in nasal tones of melancholy cadence. In the course of ten minutes she referred to three peers, her weak chest, and her constant attendance at eight o'clock Celebration. Simon thought her dull and absurd, but not hypocritical. She was too indolent to assume a virtue or affect religious airs merely to impress other people; the only creature she lived to please, to flatter, and to satisfy, was herself; and if she had once felt bored by a Feast-day, or dismayed by a Fast, she would have found chapter and verse for proving one Romish, and the other unnecessary. She had the same mannerisms in the solitude of her own room which she showed in company. "A self-deceiver," thought Warre, who began to get impatient.

At last Anne made her appearance in all the pride of a fresh and carefully studied toilette. Her hair was arranged with exquisite care, she wore a dainty bonnet, and her grey gown fell in the softest lines about her gracious figure. Her shoes, her gloves, her veil, had an elegance, a correctness which delighted the young man, who was himself fastidious in his attire—even dandified—and at an age when the decrees of fashion have a deeper meaning than the Ten Commandments. Anne's manner with Warre hovered between the bewitching shyness of a young girl who feels herself under the eyes of an admirer and the assurance of a woman of the world. Her cheeks were flushed, but the hand she gave him was firm and steady.

"I am so glad you were able to come," she said; and, with a mysterious glance which seemed to say that if the occasion for more intimate speech was not theirs at that moment, it might haply come at some future time, she began to chatter about things she had only read of and people she had never met, in that sentimental, over-earnest manner usual in young people who have spent their time in castles of their own building. Until that season Anne had been rarely in society, and all her notions of life were taken from the stage. Before she made her appearance as a singer she used to spend her few spare shillings on theatre tickets, and, from the upper circle, used to study popular actresses in their various *rôles* of love-sick Peeresses, deserted Queens, and haughty beauties. Her shallow but emotional nature was quick to accept all that was extravagant, forced, and unreal; and, when Mrs. Dane took her out into the world, she liked to think herself disillusioned because, at a few dinner-parties she attended, the lords did not hurl epigrams at each other across the table, and the ladies did not look like old pictures. As Warre listened to her artificial prattle he thought her cold, because she had never loved; cynical, because she had never been cherished; and firm, because she had not yet discovered her own weakness. His judgment, floating on the waves of her hair, lost its balance, and a fatal desire entered into his mind to help this fair soul to a right understanding of herself. Simon's imagination, now fired, was not exhausted until Anne shone out in all the glamour, the romantic fascination, the piteousness of an angelic spirit doomed to live among men and to be tempted by the powers of evil. The prudish airs she displayed when he owned to an admiration for Swinburne assisted his eager faith in her passionate purity. Like most young men of the world, he had a reverence for modest women—more particularly when they happened to be young and beautiful—which was not without a tinge of false sentiment. He was growing bewildered between respect for her innocence and an admiration for her figure, when Mr. and Mrs. Algernon Dane were announced.

Mrs. Dane was a small, once pretty woman, with the round, infantile features and soft light hair which belong to those joyous creatures who are destined to a life of serene and simple happiness. Yet in contradiction to these auspicious traits, her cheeks were thin, and her body was wasted. She had the aspect of a sick child, only the look of long endurance in her eyes was womanly. She wore dismal clothes, and was clearly not minded to display her husband's wealth in the adornment of her person. For this reason Dane rarely cared to appear in public with his wife. Every one could not know that she was a Carrigrohane, and if one did not possess that knowledge, it was quite possible, as he said, to mistake her for an under-housemaid out of situation.

Algernon himself was short, lean, and bald— an ugly man with a feverish complexion, and a leer which was only one degree more threatening than his snarl. He had a reputation for sarcastic wit, and walked on tiptoe, as though its spiritual quality gave him an airy tread. He was a barrister by profession, and a pawnbroker by instinct; but as his family had enjoyed the advantages of ill-gotten wealth for at least four generations, his acquaintances were agreed, that, although he was not, he ought to have been a gentleman. His manner on entering was a strange mixture of the important and the familiar; he lounged back in an easy-chair, talked in a loud voice, and addressed various questions to Anne without putting himself to the trouble of regarding her. Only once he gave her a swift and searching glance. Warre noticed that her replies were nervous and conciliatory. She showed an anxiety to please—a fear of offending him. The young doctor was vexed, but did not marvel that the desire of laurels without the gifts which earn them, had burnt away the wings of her spirit.

Suddenly Sir Hugh expressed surprise that Casmagni was so late.

"He will never come," said Dane; "it is much too far. He is not like Warre—he hasn't got a brougham! By-the-bye," he added, staring at Simon's chin, "when do you find a spare minute for your patients? You are always going to parties and dining with duchesses!"

Dane's vulgarity was not of that genial kind which only wakes at the sound of merriment, nor did it ever show itself in a common or unexpected way. With him it was not a misfortune, but a vice —a vice which formed the very spleen of his ill-humour. As he uttered his pleasantries, the servant entered with a telegram.

"Casmagni cannot come," said Anne, as she read it. Her lips quivered; she glanced from one to the other with a grievous smile, and then fled from the room in tears. Dane, who had plucked at her skirt as she passed by him, tightened his mouth over an oath which, being stemmed in its natural course, welled up in his eyes.

"She has been overworking," he said fiercely. "She is not fit for work. She is ruining her looks!"

Sir Hugh shook his head, and observed that Anne could never bear a disappointment. Mrs. Dane offered to follow the unhappy girl, but was restrained by Lady Delaware, who explained that sympathy only made her daughter worse, that they never noticed her, and, sighing, she assailed their patience with a long account of her own miseries. "But I have learnt to suffer in silence," she said, at last; "and although the mother's heart in me longs to offer consolation to dear Annie, I have to think of the hour when she must bear her troubles alone. I cannot be with her always, and when I am called away, I would not have her find my loss too great an affliction. Many of us forget that, when, from a purely selfish desire to make ourselves indispensable to others, we teach them to rest on our poor shifting aid in preference to that ever-present Comforter—their own conscience. I feel these things deeply!" How plausible she was!

Sarah Dane was too simple not to be impressed by these elevated sentiments, and too warm-hearted to accept them. While she was searching through her little stock of polite phrases for some coldly-sweet reply, Warre took his leave. He had descended the stairs, and reached the dim, close hall when he heard his own name spoken between a sob and a whisper. Looking up, he saw Anne. She beckoned, and he reascended the staircase. Without speaking, she opened a door which he had not observed, and he followed her into a conservatory filled with Japanese lamps and dead plants.

"What must you think of me?" she said, and began to weep bitterly. "But you do not know how hard it is to be a poor woman with rich friends—with rich, ugly, vulgar friends. They can afford to pay for happiness; they can buy it."

"You ought to have everything," said Warre, "everything."

She pretended not to hear. "And it is all so lonely," she went on. "Men do not know what loneliness means—to go up and down the dark stairs—meeting no one, to open each door and find a room full of people who do not want you—whom you do not want, to return to your own room and find it emptiest of all. Oh, my God! how wretched I am! What have I not done for companionship? For companionship even for half an hour, with long, desolate days before and afterwards!" Warre did not pay much heed to these words at the time, but later in his life they shone out in his memory in letters of lead.

"I am in great trouble. I am in great doubt

about something," she said. "If I should ask you if I might come and see you soon—perhaps, this evening—would you be angry? would you think it very strange? It is impossible to talk here. I could be at your house about nine. I must ask your advice; there is no one else. Women advise each other so badly."

"To-night at nine?" he repeated. "Would not to-morrow morning be better?"

"That may be too late," she said mysteriously.

Their eyes met, and Anne was not the first to glance away. "You are not like other men," she added; "other men would misunderstand!" And then he hated himself. Why did women always make one feel a hypocrite?

"Then let it be to-night," he said briefly, and endeavoured to look as though he saw nothing unusual in her suggestion. She pressed his hand, he left her, and in leaving was annoyed to the point of extreme pleasure at the thought that they would meet again in a few hours. She was so pretty, so miserable, so foolish, and—perhaps—so innocent. He knew that she was not a woman for whom he could feel any intense affection, yet he found it a soothing speculation to wonder whether she could ever grow to care for him. O Allegra! Allegra! Allegra! You were made *for love and to be loved, and yet you would have neither!* His aching pride took balm from the hope that Anne might be more kind. Several women had pretended tenderness, had written him passionate vows, and protested infinite devotion; but his profoundly sentimental nature had been distracted in each case by some false note in a phrase, by some awkward pose, by a flaw in the complexion. He had liked those best whom he had seen but seldom, and the faces he remembered with most pleasure were those he had studied by moonlight. But Allegra said and did all things, so it seemed to him, in harmony; there was a divine neatness in every gesture she used, every word she uttered; she had beauty, distinction, and all the fascination of her Italian birth. Above all, he was in love with her, and if for no other reason than that—if she had been plain to others, dull to others, chilling to others—she was the summer in his nature, the divinity in his life. Yet he did not know this—he only knew that Anne's advances made him remember Allegra's coldness with the more passionate regret.

He did not return home immediately, but dismissed his carriage, and walked to Lord Wickenham's. His lordship was dressing for dinner, and Warre went up to his room—a large, imposing apartment, remarkable for its bare simplicity and a four-posted bed, once pressed by the royal limbs of Queen Elizabeth. The furniture was mahogany, and the prevailing tint of things, maroon.

"Well," said Wickenham, who was attacking his close-cropped hair with two large brushes as Simon entered, "well, what have you been doing?"

Simon described his visit to the Delawares—omitting, however, his last interview with Anne—and ended with the observation: "I am sorry for that girl."

"Then don't interrupt her life," said Wickenham shortly.

"What do you mean?"

Wickenham drew himself up, and assumed the manner which, in after days, created so great an impression when he addressed the House of Lords.

"I have always held," said he, "that friendship means the bearing of confidence and not the disloading of advice. But to-day you have spoken plainly to me of a matter which to yourself is, I believe, only the vague interest of a passing hour—an emotion which will die in the utterance. I think, therefore, that I may reply as I would if we were discussing any question, which touched neither of us so deeply, that each would feel it might be more conveniently argued in the other's absence. The situation is this: you have met a woman who is young and pretty—even unusually pretty—who, you have every reason to suppose, is in circumstances of rather common unhappiness. She would be rich, but she is poor; she would be distinguished, but she is not a genius; she would be a leader of fashion, but she is not in the great world. As a man of experience, you observe that she is hysterical, vain, light-minded, but as a son of Adam you concede that her natural charms atone in a considerable degree for these intellectual defects. You feel a grinning compassion for her little woes, and a wish to amuse yourself by making her happy. And how is this to be done? By writing her empty notes for the sake of hinting at a tenderness—which you do not feel—over the signature. By paying her occasional visits, following her with your eyes when you meet, sighing when you part, and forgetting her entirely when she is not in sight. By disturbing her daily occupation with dinners, excursions up the river, suppers here, and opera-boxes there, by exposing her to the remarks of the too numerous who live by devouring reputations, and to the attentions of men who see no reason why others should fail where, as they will suppose, you have succeeded—

men who are either too wise to love her, or too mean to marry poverty. Women must either be loved or left. Leave her alone! You cannot be merely kind to her; she may grow to care for you, and, in your attempt to make her happier, you will give her pain, humiliation, misery."

"And if she did grow to care for me," said Warre, "do you think I should be such——" He stopped short and flushed—less at the thought that his friend could suspect his intentions, than at the knowledge that his own imagination—if not his will—had brooded over unutterable possibilities.

"She attracts you, but you do not love her," said Wickenham stubbornly, "and, if she loved you, it would make you wretched. You want a *bourgeois* devotion expressed in the spirit of Dante. For God's sake, leave her alone!"

"How do you know," said Warre, "that I have not some thought of asking her to marry me? A man must settle, and so long as a woman is pretty, good-humoured, and refined, what more should he want? There is nothing more," he added, in a tone of defiance. "Say what you will, there is nothing more. The rest that one hears is the stuff that dreams are made of—the language of ungratified desire. Men and women who lead natural lives have very little to offer about ideals of love

When I was very young I read the poets, and I am afraid I shall never weed their damnable poetry out of my mind. But it is all wrong, all a mistake —profoundly unhealthy. It makes one a weak fool—maudlin—a seeker after strange stars and new moons. I have imagined heroic passions which you and I would laugh at in a sick girl. Yet I know that these ordinary love affairs fill one with self-contempt—they are a weakness, a degradation of the spirit. I am wretched, however, if there is not a woman in sight. I always hope that she may be the creature I can worship. I have even seen one or two I could have loved for ever if they had only held their tongues. But there is always so much treachery—so much artifice, so much selfishness—there are always such little meannesses, so many lies. Why is it, I wonder, that there is no abiding pleasure to be found merely in the senses? Why do perishable creatures like men and women have such a longing for something eternal—something in which the senses have no share? Passion is so rich in protestations, and so frail a bond."

"I don't think that many of us are troubled by fancies of this kind," replied Wickenham. "The great thing in life is to be in earnest—say what you mean, not what you think you ought to say, and strive for the thing you want—not for the thing which the philosophy of the moment has made fashionable, or the emotion of a day has made a little tempting. There is very little poetry in me, but if I had an ideal like yours I should either stick to it or drop it altogether. If you consider it impossible, you are a fool to give it a second thought, and if it is possible, you are a coward if you accept anything less."

"Miss Delaware is a woman whom any man would admire," said Warre. "She—she is most attractive."

"I admire her extremely," said Wickenham, "but then I am a Pagan; my goddesses are always very human. I offer them sympathy rather than respect!"

CHAPTER VI

A Little Love, a Little Science

WHEN Anne entered Warre's study that evening she found him standing directly under the light, reading—or pretending to read—a book. She noticed that he was unusually pale, that he looked very grave. After the man-servant had closed the door and left them alone, she hung her head like a guilty child, and said very humbly: "It is so good of you to see me!" Warre had resolved to capture, in the coming interview, every impulse and every thought which strayed from the domain of pure and dispassionate friendship. Yet even as he heard the rustle of her silk skirts and the light fall of her feet, his heart began to beat with a force too strong for his will—with an agitation beyond the control of philosophy. Why should there always be this humiliating struggle between the flesh and the spirit? Why should he be attracted against his wish by a woman whom he did not love, when his whole mind was fixed on another?

He looked at Anne, and almost hated her extravagant prettiness, her ostentatious femininity. His conversation with Wickenham had roused a passion of remembrance—the remembrance of sweet, unearthly moments passed with Allegra—of all the romantic and chivalrous ideals he had formed of a wife, the dearest, truest, purest, man ever worshipped—of a love fresh as the blue fields of heaven, and rich with the fairest blessings of life. What was Anne to him? Nothing. Had she been an angel from Paradise, he did not want her. He pitied her, had a certain affection for her, but his mood of some hours before had passed away, even as Wickenham had warned him. All that remained was a tumult of sensation, unspeakable, disquieting; nature is not so easy a companion as false sentiment.

Anne seated herself by the table, and, placing her elbows there, rested her chin between her hands. The tears which she had shed that afternoon had only given her countenance the brilliant mistiness of an April shower, and her bright eyes shone through it like two suns. Behind her and on each side rose the long lines of bookshelves filled with ponderous and sombre volumes, whose gilt lettering, sometimes caught by the light from the pendant lamp, glittered with wise names. The velvet curtains were drawn across the window, a screen of Japanese embroidery concealed the door, the room seemed to hang somewhere out of the universe; not a sound from the outer street reached either of its two inmates; all was still.

"I am not going to cry," said Anne. "I will be very quiet, and will not waste too much of your time. This afternoon I was distressed and over-tired, and was not myself. People always say that they were not themselves when they have done anything particularly foolish! You told me that the first time I met you—when we were talking at dinner. I cannot think what makes you so kind to me. No one has ever been so kind before. I have no friends. I am only a woman who sings to the mob."

He was touched. He had seen enough of her home life to feel that there might be some truth in her words. Her character, he thought, was like an artificial arrangement of natural flowers—the roses wired, the stems composed of sticks, the whole tied up with ribbon. The emotions she displayed and the stories she told were genuine in part, but ribbon, stick, and wire were the ruling elements.

"And yet," she continued, in a low voice, "and

yet there is some one who wishes to—to help me—if I could only make up my mind that it would not be dishonourable to accept his kindness."

"Dishonourable?" asked Warre, lifting his eyebrows.

"You see," she said artlessly, "you see, I do not care for him." She looked at Simon as she spoke, and a wave of colour swept over her cheeks.

"It would be terrible," she added; "yet this life kills me. I cannot sing always, and I can only be young a little while longer. It is a choice between unhappiness in comfort and unhappiness in poverty."

"I suppose you mean," said Warre slowly, "that you have had an offer of marriage from a man you do not love?"

Anne dropped her eyes in acquiescence.

"Would it be impossible for you to care for him?"

The girl smiled bitterly, and made two attempts to speak before she answered. Shame and despair cast their shadows on her face; she held out her two hands with an appealing gesture, as though she were endeavouring to repulse a force beyond her strength.

"He is a man like Algernon Dane!" she said at last.

"Good God!" exclaimed Warre.

"How dare you look at me like that?" she cried passionately. "You do not know what it is to be poor."

"Would you sell yourself?"

The question was brutal, and her gentle, sorrowful reply filled him with remorse. "I think he loves me," she murmured; "and where there is love it seems to be a woman's part to yield, sooner or later, and to regret."

"To regret?"

"Some of us are so weak," she explained hurriedly, "and we cannot afford to despise affection. Men always say, 'I love you—give me your world.' And then the woman gives her world—and then—he puts it out of her reach for ever. Cannot you imagine a girl who has never cared for any one being touched at last by devotion, and thinking that if love is on one side at least, it is enough for happiness? And then—to meet some one else who seems so different from all the others—I forget what I was going to say. But if you tell me to break off—with this other—friend—I will do so."

"You are very inexperienced," said Warre, "too inexperienced to marry. You must wait a little."

"But men are so impatient."

Something in her tone—in the expression which flitted over her countenance as she spoke—produced an effect in his mind which was not altogether curiosity, not altogether suspicion, yet a sentiment curiously akin to both.

"What do you mean?" he asked.

"If a man wants to marry a girl like me—poor, like me, and, like me, a professional singer—he is so exceptional that he ought not to be kept waiting for an answer." Anne had changed her position, and now sat with her hands clasped in her lap, her head thrown back with an air of defiance, of contempt.

"What do you mean?" he asked again.

"I never expected any man to ask me to marry him," she replied, turning pale; "only rich girls are loved. Love is too dear for me That is why I am so grateful—oh, so grateful—for your kindness." Her voice trembled, and as she looked at Warre he saw the unmistakable light of true affection shine through her tears. She cared for him; it was a woman's way—sweet, absurd, unsought, unreasonable. He did not deserve it. Should he accept the gift, or, since he had so little to offer in return, would it not be more honest to seem harsh, unknowing, and unkind?

Had she ever looked so pretty? It should not be a hard task to like—even considerably—so bewitching a woman. She did not ask the intense love he bore for Allegra, and which Allegra valued so lightly. And a man needed more in his life than a possession which he could never call his own—a passion which could only spend itself in sighing. Yet as he remembered Allegra, in order to decide how best and most wisely he could forget her, a vision of her face came before him, and, heart-sick, he looked away from the woman at his side.

"I have not been kind," he said hurriedly; "I have not done anything to deserve your gratitude, and I am not sure that I can even give you advice worth following, or advice, at any rate, which any other man could not give equally well, and would not give quite as willingly. You make me feel wretched when you thank me for a service which costs me nothing—which is, in fact, no service at all, but a mere formal politeness."

At that moment his servant entered with the letters which had arrived by the last post, and Warre was thankful for the interruption. While the man was present he glanced at Anne more easily, and smiled at her with frank friendship;

but no sooner had he left them than the old embarrassment returned, a stifling oppression was in the atmosphere. Anne said nothing; he could only hear her delicate, quick breathing, which reminded him of a child asleep. The air seemed to have caught the vibration of her heart.

He turned over the letters; one bore the Roman postmark and Allegra's prim little handwriting.

"Will you excuse me?" he said unsteadily. "This is the only one which is important. I can look at the others later," and walked away. Anne could not see him; he pressed the envelope to his lips, covered it with kisses, broke the seal. And it contained six lines of formal thanks for a rosary of pearls he had sent her for a birthday gift. He was most kind. She remained sincerely his, Allegra Vendramini.

He burst out laughing, crumpled the letter in his hand, and flung it into the grate. "Dear little girl," he said to Anne, "who would not be kind to you? You have a heart." He stooped, kissed her once, kissed her again, saying to himself, "I do not love you in the least," but owning that her cheeks were pleasant.

> "Lovely Thaïs sits beside thee,
> Take the good the gods provide thee!"

Hateful couplet! Sound philosophy! "Anne, do

you like me a little?" he cried. "I believe you do. How sweet you are! Give up that other brute and marry me. I can give you everything! I will take care of you! You shall never again have a wish, a whim, one delightful, foolish, womanly desire ungratified. Isn't life splendid? Isn't it a gift? Isn't it glorious? Oh, tell me again you care for me!"

She seized his hand and kissed it passionately. "I love you! Oh, I love you!" she repeated. "I cannot tell you why, but I do." All her nature was in the cry. The love she felt was not that of a woman who had thought much, who either bestowed, or demanded, or understood a great passion, but it was graceful, winning, and full of that caressing, rather animal, tenderness which, until it palls, is so seductive. The truth is always sobering, and the honesty of Anne's commonplace affection made Warre ashamed.

"I will write to you to-morrow," he said; "you shall never regret having cared for me. Dear little lady, good-night!" He fastened her mantle at the throat, and with his arm round her waist led her to the door.

"Good-night! good-night! Are you happy, darling, are you happy? We must be married soon. Will you be happy with me?"

"So happy," said Anne.

"And you like me . . . a little?"

She leaned her head against his breast and wept; clung to him, kissed him timidly. Who would not be kind to her? She had a heart . . .

He put her into a cab, and watched it roll away into the night. She was going to Mrs. Dane's. When he returned to the study his eyes fell on Allegra's letter, which lay where he had tossed it, in the grate. And he picked it up that he might have the misery of hurling it from him once more "That is ended," he said. "Ended! ended! for ever ended!"

As Anne drove away, she thought how comfortable Warre's house was, how agreeable it would be to live there, and how much she loved him. She did not consider him handsome; his good looks were of a type which she did not understand. She liked something more conventional—more effective, in fact. But he was very nice, and what lovely Persian carpets! What fine pictures on the staircase! He surely made a lot of money. And he was no doubt generous. The servant looked contented. Oh, Simon was charming! She loved him dearly. She hoped the drawing-room was large. All the interesting people in London would come and see them. She would have a great wedding, for, of course, he meant to marry her. He had told her to break off with the other brute. And the other was a brute. She hated him. But he had given her some beautiful presents Would she be obliged to send them back?

The Danes' mansion in Portland Place had been furnished to resemble as closely as possible the dwellings of the great, as they are shown on the stage of fashionable theatres. This, however, was not Sarah's ordering, but her husband's; the poor lady suffered in that upholstered Eden. She received Anne in her boudoir—a room which had been arranged with uncomfortable luxury in the falsely Oriental style, and which formed the most inappropriate background conceivable for the dowdy little woman who spent her time there. Goldfish sported in an alabaster fountain near the lattice window; a crystal lamp hung over the low couch; palm and bamboo trees, tiger-skins and embroidered cushions, were scattered here and there with studied negligence; an ivory statuette of the *Diana* of Bernini and a bad copy of Botticelli's Virgin were placed, one on a gorgeous pedestal of malachite and lapis lazuli, the other on a richly carved gilt easel. A painted screen containing photographs of the Carrigrohane family shielded Sarah from the draught; a fur footstool in white fox kept her feet warm. An odour of musk and cedar-wood filled the apartment. Mrs. Dane was clothed in a tea-gown of slate-coloured cashmere, trimmed with quilted satin. She wore a white lace frill sewn in the neck of this garment, and a dreadful pearl brooch, in the shape of a true lovers' knot, was fastened at her throat, pricking her chin when she moved. It would never have entered her head to pin the atrocious ornament a hair's-breadth lower; she had the martyr's instinct. She lifted her tired eyes as Anne entered, gave her a cold, thin hand, and motioned her to a seat near her own. She was a little deaf.

Anne's senses were in that state of exaltation which not only deprived her of the power of speech but of all desire to talk. Women of indolent and selfish nature are rarely communicative until they have exhausted the joy of silent imagination, and even then they tell very few of their intimate thoughts. Anne sat down by her friend, threw back her head with a sigh of infinite content, and waited to be entertained. What room, she wondered, in Warre's house could serve as a boudoir? She would have it prettier than Sarah's. She did not admire this so much as usual. It did not seem so extraordinarily magnificent. Other men besides Dane could afford to give their wives beautiful things.

"You look much better than you did this afternoon," said Sarah suddenly. " I was quite anxious. You need not have been so annoyed about that tiresome Casmagni. I never care for Italians, and Algernon hates music. We went to see you, dear, not any one else. What did it matter to us whether Casmagni came or not? You are too modest."

"Am I?" said Anne, who was already thinking how little she needed Casmagni now. She would offer him a fee to sing at one of her later receptions; their acquaintance in future should rest on a coldly professional basis. She would remember every one who had been kind to her when she was poor, but most of all, those who had been unkind—who had treated her as an inconsiderable person.

Sarah took up some knitting and made a few dull remarks about her plans for the summer, the Duchess of Wark's increasing grey hairs, the crush at Lady Windegrave's. And what a pity it was that the Maukin-Fawkeses had no family. Women with children were the happiest. They had a larger store of affection than men, and needed more creatures to love. A great many women died just from hoarding devotion.

" I am the oldest creature I ever met," she said. Anne made no reply, but stared back. Sarah surveyed the radiant face before her, and sighed bitterly. "I have been cheated out of my youth," she said. "Beauty is only given to few, but every one that is born has at least the right to be young. I never had a frolic in my life; I do not even know the pleasure of giggling. When I hear girls giggle it makes me envious. Oh, it is too hard! Why did they make me marry? I know that there were eight of us at home, but I was not very much in the way. I gave as little trouble as I could." The work dropped from her fingers and rolled to the ground. "I'm rather upset," she continued. "Algernon told me at dinner—he dined at home this evening, as he has a headache, and feels too stupid to go out—Algernon told me that Boteler is going to divorce his wife. Poor woman!"

"Why *poor* woman?" said Anne indignantly. "Boteler gave her six hundred a year for her dress, and although she hates the river, that was a splendid steam-launch he had built for her birthday!"

"He is a bad husband," replied Sarah, "and her child died. I daresay her heart was broken before she ran away with Drawne."

"Women cannot always plead that they have worthless husbands, or that their children are dead," said Anne, who, with respectable prosperity before her eyes, felt an intolerance of sin and sinners, which she had never known before. "Some women are merely vain and some merely vicious, and some . . . merely desperate."

"I daresay," said Sarah, "but I am sorry for them nevertheless—oh, so sorry for them. Men do not care for a dull, plain little woman like me, so I have never been tempted. But if I were, I have no reason to think that I should be any stronger than the rest."

"Were you never in love," asked Anne.

"Oh yes, but that was long ago. He was poor, and I knew that if he married at all, he would have to choose a woman with money. You see, it was hopeless from the beginning; so he told me he loved me, and I told him I loved him, and we kissed each other good-bye. That was all that happened. It is a very short story to tell, but it's my whole life, Anne. All the rest is merely time—time—just hours, weeks, and months. We won't talk of that; I have something else to say—I want to ask you a question."

"A question?" said Anne, with a look of terror.

"I want you to tell me your secret."

The girl grew white; when she spoke her voice was trembling. "My secret? I have no secret, Mrs. Dane."

6

"But it is written in your eyes. Ah, don't be frightened. I am the only one who can read them."

"What do you see there?"

"A lover!" said Sarah. "Ah! you cannot deny it. Why have you tried to deceive me? I knew it all from the first. He betrayed himself. You were more demure."

Anne stood up; she was shivering, ghastly. She seemed enveloped in a white flame which burnt and burnt without destroying, only leaving her powerless to move or utter a cry. What did Sarah know? What would she do? Her heart ceased to beat; the ground seemed to rock under her feet; the room floated before her eyes like a stifling vapour.

"If you must say it, say it quickly," she murmured. "I am not a coward."

"You are desperately in love with him, and have not the courage to own it."

"My God, no!" cried Anne. "No! No! That is the worst of it. I hate him! I hate him! That is the worst of it. Be merciful!"

"To-day you touched his glove when it was lying on the table," said Sarah. "That did not look like hatred. Here it is; I stole it for you. What would my husband say if he knew I had Dr. Warre's glove next my heart!"

"*Warre's* glove!" exclaimed Anne, the colour rushing back into her cheeks. "*Warre's* glove. You meant *Warre*." She laughed, and laughed, and laughed; threw herself on the sofa, laughing. "*Warre's* glove! *Warre's* glove!"

"Own that I was right, and you shall have it."

"Give it to me!"

Sarah was laughing now with real childish merriment. What fun it was to tease Anne! She was so emotional. It was as good as a play. "Own that you have fallen in love with him, and you shall have it!" she said. "Own——" Neither of them heard Algernon Dane enter the room. He came forward with his curious mincing step, looking from one to the other in astonishment.

"How merry we are!" he said, with his unpleasant smile.

"We are playing a game, that is all," said his wife, still tittering.

"What game?" he asked.

"Thought-reading," answered Anne, who had grown very quiet.

"And I scared her," said Sarah gaily. "Don't you think she must have some terrible secret? Ah!

I shall soon get so wise that you will all turn pale when you hear me coming."

Algernon forced a laugh and left them. It was known that he had a contempt for the society of virtuous women.

CHAPTER VII

A Soliloquy during the Small Hours

WARRE slept little that night. He would close his eyes for a few moments and lose himself in formless regions, listening to a far-off language which seemed an echo of words he had forgotten; but it was only to wake again in a world of cutting distinctness, and to hear thoughts he understood too well. A feverish longing to be at peace possessed his spirit. Work seemed to absorb all that was steady, immutable, and sane in his nature; he could only be sure of his judgment in matters connected with his profession. He knew that his mind was not well balanced: in one scale there was a force and weight which sometimes astonished himself; in the other, a feather-light heap of impulses, whims, and follies, of resisted temptations, of despised opinions—the refuse of a character. What did it all mean? Brain fag? The damnable poetry he had read in his youth? An undisciplined imagination? A romantic temperament? The desire for something more than creature comforts and animal satisfaction? Why could he not be happy? Why this torturing disquietude, these moods of self-contempt, this remorse for sins he had never committed, this despairing grief for a loss he had never suffered, this ceaseless watching for a joy which never came, this weary search for a treasure which could not be found, this longing for things he could not define? And it had always been so; neither gratified ambition, nor money, nor amusements, could please him long; his affection for Wickenham was the only abiding sentiment in his life. It was certainly a constant—if not intoxicating—pleasure to think of Wickenham; to admire his sturdy, unassailable convictions; his honest Pagan heart. Yet even Wickenham was not a happy man; he never complained, never whined, never showed discontent; but he lived under the restraint of a strange, unaccountable sadness. What did it mean? Did Wickenham, too, have an ideal?

Warre roused himself from these vain speculations by laughing aloud at the foolishness of two able-bodied young men, like himself and his friend, growing sentimental, making themselves wretched because the gifts of life were not the gifts of a

Heaven which no mortal had ever inhabited. He took courage, and faced the thought of Anne and the letter he must write to her on the morrow. She was very pretty—adorably pretty. She was fond of him. How difficult to grant this, and not feel himself a coxcomb! How charming she was! How lucky any man was to win even a little of her affection! What a brute, what a poor stick he would be not to thrill with gratitude for such a gift. God forbid that he should under-estimate Anne's sweetness. He did not deserve it; but henceforth it should be his task to prove himself a shade less unworthy. Love was too rare a thing to be lightly valued. There was no gainsaying that beautiful expression in her eyes. He was at last dear to some one; some one loved him purely simply, childishly. He was tired of passionate amours. That was why he had thought so seriously of marriage lately. That was why he had so nearly lost his head about . . . that little girl . . . in Rome. The recollection of Allegra plucked like a hand at his heart. He might sneer at his weakness, but the truly excellent can never satiate—never lose its sway over the affections of men and women. Warre could not persuade himself that the feeling which drew him towards Allegra was but a sentimental sensuality—a mood born of that craving for an amorous adventure which steals over the strongest and wisest with an intensity exactly commensurate with their strength and wisdom. But she was the embodiment of all the romantic dreams of his boyhood and youth : the being he had sought in every heroine, the Beatrice, the Francesca, the Lady Hamilton, the Juliet, the Mary of his imagination. She had taught him that his fancy did not lie. The woman he had conjured up from the delicious mist and vague of chivalrous tales, religious fancies, heroic lives, and immemorial legends really lived. The poets and lovers of history had written no falsehoods, cherished no vain illusions. Was it not something —nay, everything—to have learnt this? And if he might never look on Allegra again, never again hear the music of her voice, never feel the innocent witchery of her eyes, the inspiration of her presence, he had at least once seen her, once spoken with her face to face, loved her then, and now loved her for all time.

But Anne ?

Should he mope for the unattainable, and spend his days in melancholy solitude ? This would be neither manly nor Dantesque. He would marry —not to find forgetfulness, but that remembrance might be less bitter. . . Anne was plainly a domestic woman—one who would take an absorbing concern in her home, her husband, her children, dinner-giving, the management of servants, the paying and receiving of afternoon calls. She had all the sound feminine instincts. Heaven be praised! she was not artistic. The dust of Bohemianism she had gained from her brief pilgrimage in the musical world could be brushed off in a day. And she looked like a princess in a fairy tale. What a jewel he had found, to be sure! She was a good little creature, too. In passing an ivory crucifix which he had bought in Rome, she, not knowing that he could see her, had kissed it devoutly. A wife should be, above all things, religious. He would love her for her piety. It was amazing that she had kept either her faith or her innocence in that miserable boarding-house, in the pitiable struggle for a small success, with that whining, self-deceived mother. And who was the man like Algernon Dane? Could it be a relative of Dane's? Dane's manner with Anne was certainly rather offensive . . . there was a nameless . .

The night was long. If there had only been Anne to think of, how soon he could have fallen asleep. She touched his interest so lightly. It was not easy to put her out of his mind, because it required such an effort of will to keep her there. Choosing a wife was a business, a labour, a disheartening task. He had made his choice. He would marry Anne, and leave the rest to the gods. Once a husband, he would try to convince himself that ceaseless yawning was the fit and peaceful occupation of a satisfied soul; he would make friends again with his books, try to spin his life out of the old dull threads . . . and work.

Work!

And alas! he was so tired of work. Oh, to escape for one enchanted moment into that undiscovered country whose sapphire rivers flow through gardens of oleander and idleness, and where the willows sigh in the scent-laden winds; where the acacia spreads her delicate lace against an azure sky; where light is the betrothal of the moon's silver and the sun's gold. There to lie on the flower-sweet grass and watch the deathless nymphs dance a perpetual youth, to countless time, in robes of ever-varying hue, to music of ever-changing harmony, to the murmur of insects and the song of the nightingale; to drive white oxen down the long avenues of ilex, or wander through vineyards where the air would be sleepy like wine and the fragrance heavy with oblivion. O undiscovered country! Why is it so easily imagined? Why would it be so impossible to live there—and be happy?

Morning came, and with it an awakening to things real, to the blessed necessity of striving with other minds than one, of considering other problems than those egoistic.

"Thank God," cried Warre, "there is my work! That is the one abiding solace! But, Allegra, if you had only cared for me . . . a little!"

CHAPTER VIII

Contrition in the Robust

WHEN Anne arose that same day, it was some hours later, and after a night of untroubled repose. Her little room was on the attic-floor, and through the one small window, which was cut high near the sloping ceiling, she could see the black roofs of the neighbouring houses, their chimneys spouting smoke, and the sky. Here and there the spire of a church thrust its point into the horizon, and, far away to the left, there was a mews where every tiny casement over each stable door had its ledge packed with pots of geranium, creeping Jenny, and blossomless rose-trees. Sometimes a coachman's wife would appear above them, calling to her man below, or to her children playing in the yard; one could hear voices, laughter, swearing, cries, the clatter of feet on the stone-paving, and the trample of horses, their neighing, and the crack of whips. One woman sang; her clear, fresh notes had the tone of the country and the woods and the birds. But her songs were all about "*booze*," and two lovely black eyes, and the pal who had had a bit of money left him. . . . Anne's iron bed was covered with a patchwork quilt made from cotton stuffs cut out in clumsy diamonds; a square of faded matting was spread in the centre of the floor, the boards around were bare. A zinc bath, a pierglass, and a wash-hand-stand of painted deal formed the sole furniture. The girl used to open her eyes each morning, survey the meagre scene with disgust, and say : " How long? " To-day she awoke smiling. Poor little room! She would be almost sorry to leave it. If Simon came to see her that day, it would not be until the afternoon. If he wrote, she could not receive the letter for some hours. How could she kill the time? Ordinarily, she would have sung her scales, read the newspaper, and walked in the Row. But she would save the Row for the morrow, when Warre could accompany her. What fun it would be to see amazement on all the faces she was so heartily sick of—and yet feared! In the meantime, however, why not go to church? It would be a nice thing to tell Simon when he came or when she answered his letter. "*Darling*," she would say, "*when I was in church this morning, I could not keep my thoughts from*

wandering to you. I hope this was not wicked?"
Besides, it would please God. He had been very kind to her, after all, and . . . she had not been . . . devout . . . lately.

During the service—and being a week-day it was short—she applied herself with diligence to every prayer, with her eyes fixed in an ecstasy on the altar, her hands clasped in fervour. She had never felt so happy, nor so eager to do right, to excel in all the virtues. She was deeply sorry for all her transgressions; her life in the future would be different. She asked for strength to keep her pious resolutions, praying very amiably for such blessings as might be *good* for Simon and her parents, and got up from her knees in that condition of bodily peace and serenity which is more often the portion of a healthy sinner than a penitent soul

Algernon Dane was standing in the porch.

"What in the world is this new fancy?" said he, "all this mewing and praying? I saw you leave the house, and I followed you here. But what does it mean? What does it amount to? For goodness' sake give it up. It is so depressing . . . your look is enough to freeze one. Religion does not suit you. I have been watching you for the last half hour, and I never saw such a performance in my life. A dying duck!"

Anne walked silently beside him until they reached a corner of the street, when, evidently following a habit, they turned into a dismal road lined with leafless trees, and houses with gardens of dead evergreens.

"You always sneer at me," said the girl, "when I try to get above my mud-heap. But I have done with you. You and I can have nothing more to say to each other. Now let me go."

"Where are you going?" asked Dane. "Who is going to pay your bills?"

A woman who could have so gross an insult offered her, even by such a man as Dane, would not be the woman to feel it. Anne accepted it with serenity. "I have changed," she said.

"You are in love with Warre!" shouted Dane. "Do you think I have been fooled for one instant? I know you too well, my girl! Warre's girl! Any man's girl!"

"You are very rude and very unkind."

"You deserve it," he said, "although I do not wish to abuse you. But I am not a saint, and when I see you with these righteous airs it is more than I can stand. You are no better than I am—not a whit better."

"That is the worst of it," she replied. "But I

see that I have been wrong. I feel it. You do not see your dishonour?"

"Oh yes, I do," he said. "I know a lot of people who would call me a blackguard."

"Why don't you try and lead a better life?"

"I will, if I can find some pretty woman to say prayers with me. I know the sort of hypocrisy—talking over the six deadly sins and looking a seventh. Bah! Women like you always reform when there is a rich husband in sight. They begin to long for the peaceful joys of domesticity. I respect these penitents who leave one man because he is a sinner, to deceive another because he is a saint. Oh, Anne, I know you so well!"

He looked at her as he spoke, and studied, in an agony of admiration, her delicate profile, the fresh and child-like lips, the arched eyebrows and glistening hair. She was tall, with divine shoulders; there was an elegant defiance in her gait. He knew of no marble goddess so imposing, so beautiful, so alluring. And he had been a great traveller; had seen a lot of women . . . purchased many works of art.

"Come," he said hoarsely, "make it up. I would have bought you that tiara long ago, but I was afraid all the old cats would talk. They will forgive a few smart dresses, but they won't stand diamonds. They would say it wasn't all done by singing. I was only thinking of your reputation; I never see any harm in anything . . . what were we born for? It's so natural to love a pretty woman. I'm prepared to go to any length . . . I'll settle something handsome on Sarah; give her the Portland Place house for life, and take you abroad. I will make any sacrifice to please you. I did not know that you were so keen on the tiara. You cannot say that I have ever denied you anything. Come back into the church and talk things over. It is beginning to rain. Where's the umbrella I gave you last week? I knew you would like that handle . . . tortoiseshell and emeralds. I have been kind to you, haven't I? Three or four women have been making up to me lately—titled women, too, but I have put them off."

They entered the church. One old man was praying in a remote corner; otherwise it was empty. The greyness, the cold, and the silence were horrible to Dane.

"There's only one way to go to church," he said, and that's in a coffin. I wish it would stop raining. It's warmer outside."

Anne, as though she had not heard him and was even unaware of his presence, knelt down. Where had she learnt this composure? Her face was as calm as a medallion of the Virgin which decorated a memorial-tablet on the wall over her head. She seemed in a stupor of happiness.

"Say something!" exclaimed Dane.

"I have nothing to say. And I cannot listen to you here. You forget where we are."

"No, I don't. I have kissed you by that pillar many times."

"I have changed," she repeated, and read her Prayer-Book. An amethyst bracelet, which Dane had given her in the first days of their acquaintance, dropped from her wrist. He picked it up and put it into his own pocket.

"That's mine!" he said.

Anne showed no surprise, felt none. She was no critic in matters of conduct, and was as incapable of despising a meanness as she was of appreciating a chivalrous sentiment. She coloured with annoyance, however, that Dane had been, as it were, too clever for her. But he laughed aloud himself, and, as she was good-humoured, the corner of her mouth trembled a little in sympathy. The strongest link between them was a common desire for gain, for making a shrewd bargain, for getting more, if possible, than one's money's worth out of life. Theirs was the Gospel of Give and Take.

Anne threw Dane a glance which was a compound of congratulation and envy. Now, he thought, they were beginning to understand each other once more. She would soon come round. There was nothing like letting a woman know that one had a certain amount of proper pride, of self-respect; that one would not be treated like a dog. And yet ... that implacable rose-leaf countenance. And that eternal praying. He touched her arm, and grew faint, sick, deathlike at the mere contact.

"If you want to flirt with Warre," he murmured, getting hoarse, "I won't be unreasonable about it. I won't ask any questions ... he isn't worth a quarrel. But he won't be generous   he's too young and good-looking ... he thinks that generosity isn't necessary. He doesn't understand women."

"He has asked me to marry him," said Anne, stung into defending her market value.

He looked incredulous, derisive. "I believe that," he observed drily. Why did she always invent such silly lies?

"If I were going to tell a lot of beastly falsehoods," he said, "I swear I wouldn't do it in church and over a Prayer-Book. That is going a little too far, even for me. And I'm not a Pharisee.

Of course, girls always want to make out that somebody is dying to marry them. That's an old trick . . . it only deceives boys. As if a fellow like Warre would choose you for his wife, my dear. I wouldn't do that myself, and I am very fond of you!"

"What is there against me?" she asked. His face was convulsed with a terrible smirk; he dropped his eyes discreetly.

"I have told him all about you," said Anne.

Dane sprang to his feet, livid with fear, with rage, with disappointed passion. "What?" he said, "what? You have betrayed me?"

"I managed it very well," replied Anne. "I did not mention names. I am much too fond of poor Sarah to do anything of that kind!"

"You are a very wicked woman," said Dane, whimpering with relief, "and you can go to the devil. I don't want you. Go, for God's sake, go!"

Anne stood up. Lifting her skirt from the dust, she tripped delicately past him—without a glance . . without a gesture, and out of the church.

"Go!" repeated Dane, but in a weaker voice. With a vacant stare, he watched the swinging door through which she had vanished, and which still trembled on its hinges . . . wailing . . . creaking.

He summoned up his strength for a cry which she could not hear, and shouted again :

"Go, for God's sake!"

Then, on tiptoe, he stole into another aisle where there was an old-fashioned pew with curtains. And there he hid himself to weep . . and curse.

CHAPTER IX

Mortal Happiness

AFTER those ashen hours before dawn, and until the instant when Warre ascended the staircase which led to the drawing-room in Southwick Terrace, he had not suffered himself to think again of Anne or of what he should say when they met. Was it because he would have found no pleasure in the anticipation? The unknown prospect lay before his mind, like the scene, which, on entering a theatre, one knows must shortly be discovered by the curtain. And now that the appointed time was come for the uplifting of that veil, he felt an indifference so terrible, that, when the servant opened the door, and he saw Anne standing by the piano, her face pale with emotion and its pallor intensified by the scarlet dress she wore, he seemed to be looking at a stranger.

"Is it you?" she said, and came towards him with both hands held out—a pretty, begging gesture instinctive and unstudied—symbolic of much that was to come in their two lives. Self-confidence had given her prettiness a more severe character ... the arrogant calm which is sometimes mistaken for moral grandeur. She possessed that profane beauty which entrances every sense and afflicts the soul with a dream-troubled sleep out of which it tries to wake, and may not; from the lethargy of which it tries to rouse and remember ... warnings once heard ... resolves once taken ... and cannot. Warre took her white hands and looked, without speaking, into her unreadable blue eyes.

"Is it you?" she repeated again.

"I suppose so," he said, with an ironical smile. It was that brief moment of self-condemnation which makes the first second and the last of every foolish hour. And the period which passes between those two throbs of time may not be the sixty minutes of human counting, but a whole youth— a manhood. Anne wore a bunch of heliotrope in her belt, and its perfume drenched the commonplace room with a languid, cloying sweetness. Sunlight and dust streamed in through the open windows, and, now here and now far away, the ponderous, incessant rumble of wheels on the Uxbridge Road gave a deeper tone to the hum which is never absent from the noisy air of a great city. They were repairing the pavement and the street below, and the sharp kiss of hammer and stone, of pickaxe and ground, made a sort of barbarous music—*a clash, a clang, a cry—a cry, a clang, a crash,* wailing, monotonous—fit, inharmonious tune of those who would mend and patch an earth so impatient under men's labour.

"What are you thinking of?" asked Anne. "You said you would write, but I hoped you would come—I hoped you would wish to see me. I wanted to see you. . . . What are you thinking of?"

"Am I thinking?" he replied. "I feel as though I had forgotten everything."

"Ah!" she exclaimed, with womanly delight, "do you love me so much as that?"

He made no answer, but took her in his arms and kissed the question from her lips. "Never ask me," he said, at last, "never ask me whether I care for you. I am not a man who—says a great deal." He walked away to the sofa, and Anne seated herself at his feet, with her head against his knees.

"We must be the happiest people in the world," she murmured. "I can hardly believe that this is all true . . . that it is really happening . . . that we have met and loved each other, and are going to be married . . . going to be together always . . . that we are to be everything to each other . . . everything. It is a miracle, it frightens me. Oh, I never thought that life could be so wonderful! I have never loved any one before . . . it is all so new to me, but you . . . you are a man . . . you are older than I am . . . you have had more time. . . . There must have been several."

"There was one," said Warre, "there was one I loved very much. But it was not like this . . . not like my affection for you . . . something quite different."

"Did she die?" asked Anne, "or was she a married woman? These flirtations with married women never make men happy. I have often heard that. I wonder why people begin them!"

"She is not dead and she is not married," said Warre, "but I am not likely to see her again—at least, for some years!"

"We need not talk about her any longer," said Anne, with a pang of sudden, inexplicable jealousy; "she doesn't matter. The afternoon is going. Tell me why you love me? Tell me what first made you care for me? Did you think I was pretty?"

"Very pretty, dear," he said, "very pretty."

And he turned away from the intense glance of her eyes, for they wearied him. She drew nearer and spoke in a softer voice.

"We are both young," she whispered, "and we have a long, long life before us. Years and years. And we shall be so happy. You will tell me all your thoughts and I will tell you mine. We shall live for each other. What are you thinking of now? You seem to be always thinking. And you look over there. Look at me. Don't you like my dress? I could not wear anything dark to-day, although I know men admire black dresses. But I only want to see bright things—I wanted to think of summer. The house is sombre enough: even with you by my side it is hard to be cheerful here. And I was so anxious to look nice . . . to please you. . . . Clouds soon come. No one is happy long. There is always something."

Warre had only heard her indistinctly: it seemed a vague lament in the distance. The woman he had wished to make glad was already complaining, already uttering bitter words, already drooping in discontent and disappointment.

"But you are lovely," he exclaimed, "your dress is charming! When Dante first saw Beatrice she wore scarlet." And he remembered his meeting with Allegra in the great, desolate salon of the

Palazzo Vendramini; that long, strange, wondering look into each other's eyes; the blush on Allegra's face; then that speechless separation which now seemed irrevocable because only one had known its grief: only one had felt despair—that tearless, white despair which falls on the shoulders like a mantle of stone—for ever cold, never more to be thrown aside. It fell so lightly at first, almost like snow . . . or did it stun, and for that reason seem nothing till consciousness returned? And now . . . *this.* Perfume of heliotrope, rustle of scarlet silk, the point of a little slipper worked in beads; dust and sunlight pouring in at the window (oh, how suggestive of life!), hideous chintz on the walls; that clash, that clang, that cry of pickaxe, hammer, and stone, and Anne, young, fragrant, living, heavenly beautiful, speaking words of human love! If she would only promise not to question, not to think, or wonder. What should it matter to her what was passing in his soul! He would give her his name, his home, his worldly possessions; he would save her from labour and sorrow, care for her always, but his thoughts were his own, his memories his own, his regrets—his dreams, his own!

"Dear," he said, "if I ever seem silent, or cold, or melancholy, you must try to forgive it. A man with a profession has many things to make him troubled, to make him anxious—which sympathy cannot lessen, and which, in any case, will not bear defining. They are mists that fall on the mind—mists."

"But why have you got this mood to-day?" cried Anne. She stood up, hurt, and frowning. "Why have you got this mood to-day?" she repeated; "is it my fault?"

"It is my own accursed disposition," he said. "Come! help me to forget it."

The girl sat down by his side and put her arms round him with that protective, almost maternal tenderness which is seldom entirely absent from the love even of the coldest women. Anne had much passion of the calculating and deliberate kind, but very little affection, very little generosity, very little sweetness in her nature. What she possessed, however, she gave to Warre. He was rich, he was good-looking, he was clever, he was kind; she believed he admired her to frenzy; that he was desperately in love with her. Sometimes she had found herself wondering whether she would not have liked him almost as well if he had been quite poor . . . a mere clerk in the City. He could have tempted her to enter into a foolish marriage . . . she would have regretted it bitterly, but for a time . . . possibly for a whole year ... it might have seemed worth many sacrifices. He was not an ordinary man ... he was not so suspicious—he was much more easily deceived. Yet not a fool! She hated fools. They were so cruel . . so spiteful.

"I love you!" she exclaimed. "I love you! You are so good to me! ... I love you!"

Where there was so much beauty, and so much charm, and so much delicate abandon, who would not feel a kindling of every lover-like emotion? Anne's embrace gave Warre no happiness, no peace of mind, but it was a certain pleasure ... sensuous, beguiling ... something infinitely more agreeable, for instance, than sitting alone in his study, longing vainly for the sight of a face, which, after all, had never smiled more than a pale friendliness at him. Anne caught his hand, covered it with passionate kisses. "And now," she said, "let us talk about ourselves. And about the wedding, and the people we must invite to it. Will Lord Wickenham lend us his place at Weyborough for the honeymoon?"

He laughed a little, and deluded himself by trying to feel that they were contemplating a future which would never dawn, discussing events which by no possibility could ever come to pass. This was a fantastic comedy—a thing of no significance, and which could not last. With this false belief to still his reason, he was able to display an enthusiasm which delighted the young girl. What power she had over him! How she could charm away his moods! They invented imaginary interviews between this friend and that on the subject of the marriage : how one would sneer, and another croak, and a third—merely out of contrariety—applaud. What fun it would be! What endless fun!

"Great fun!" said Warre.

Then she grew serious. An instinct warned her that he was not a man to encourage in any flippant view of their betrothal.

"You know," she said suddenly, "your offer and your love mean more to me than an engagement ring. To every woman the prospect of a home is most alluring, but to one who has had to fight with poverty . . . who has suffered. Oh, Simon, if anything should come between us! Think what it would mean. To have known happiness, to have had it within one's grasp, and then to go back again to the old temptations . . . the old privations and humiliations. . . . I could not! I could not! Oh, never disappoint me! When I once lose faith in men, I shall lose faith in God, for they are His witnesses!"

To what degree was this strange being sincere? From the depth of her transient emotions she would sometimes utter the sentiments of no common mind, no simply animal heart, no merely airy soul. Warre that day believed in her utterly, and at no time could he ever bring himself to regard her as an incorrigible impostor. She had a nature of strong impulses, a defective education in weak principles, and that excitable temperament which needs every bodily satisfaction to keep it sane. In the absence of material aids there is only one intellectual gift which can save either men or women of this type from complete degradation, and that is a desire for romance, for refinement, for the poetic. And Anne was a stranger to this purifying influence. She had that appalling brutality of mental constitution which is more often found in creatures of delicate appearance and great nervous force than in those whose even health and robust air are the effect —less than the cause—of their tranquil spirit. Culture may do much, but nothing can alter the quality of one's moral fibre; if it be coarse, it must remain coarse, and although it may be spun into silk, it will be silk of harsh grain—unyielding, rough. Anne had no innate ideal of conduct to make her suffer when she fell beneath it; she lived by impulse—if a good one, it was well; if a bad one, it was well also. She only felt remorse when an action turned to her disadvantage, or when some adverse judgment from a looker-on wounded her self-esteem. Vanity was all the conscience she possessed; and this, although Warre did not know it then, was why it was so utterly impossible to love her, so hard even to admit her beauty without a certain reluctance, to even touch her without an inward shrinking—a sort of shame. In vain he stifled this instinct, and, although he thrust it aside, not so much as guessing, though never so dimly, what it could mean, it kept him irritable, dissatisfied, and wretched, even when he told himself—as he did that afternoon—that he was contented, far more contented, than he had ever believed it possible to be. But he looked at her fair, weak countenance, and what he lacked in love he trebly gave in sympathy, in a nameless feeling which he could not analyse, but which he knew in after years was mainly pity, partly an unwholesome fascination. Anne was not born for civilisation, for the life of towns, for the restraints imposed by considerations of religion, wealth, or custom; but for the free and heedless existence of those eternal mortals who dwelt for a brief space in fabulous

Eden. There, among birds and flowers and fruit, with one faithful and comely companion, without rivals to stir her jealousy or friends to give her advice, she would have passed transparent nights and radiant days; she would have loved the inconceivable Adam; she would have been blameless always. . . .

"How could I deceive you?" asked Warre. "How could I willingly disappoint you?" He addressed the question to his own heart, but Anne answered.

"Why do men ever deceive the women who trust them?" she said, pressing her cheek against his shoulder. "I want you to know the truth about me. I have a temper, and I am jealous. I have flirted a little, too. Once I was almost engaged; but I have told you about that, and now you know everything."

Warre laughed at this childish confession. What simplicity! What innocence!

"Did I tell you," he said, "that I called at the Bank this morning and saw your father? He was somewhat surprised to see me."

"I hope he did not talk about settlements and tedious things like that," said Anne.

"It will be all right," replied Warre, "we agreed splendidly."

The interview had been a strange one. The baronet had shown great astonishment at the idea that any man should wish to marry his daughter. He pointed out with blunt kindness that he himself could not give her a penny. She sometimes earned a handsome fee for singing, and this she spent in cab-fares and finery.

"Anne likes to gad," he said, "and although I do not approve of so young a girl rushing about London without her mother, what is one to do? I know that my sisters were not brought up that way, but they are dead—one was an old maid and the other was obliged to divorce her husband. A sad case! Poor Minnie! Besides, I must have some peace of my life; I cannot wear myself out giving advice which is never followed, and which, after all, may not be particularly good. Anne and her mother have rows, but then women are only happy when they are making each other miserable. If you marry Anne, I daresay she will turn out as good a wife as another. It's all a chance. Sometimes the most unlikely matches turn out uncommonly well. . . . Angels very often have a tongue with a tang . . . you get one of these nagging wives! I never heard Anne nag, but that is a habit which comes. Perhaps if one took it in time. . . . But if I were a single man, I should not be in a hurry to settle."

These restless phrases seemed to drop from a mind which was flying very far from the subject under consideration. Warre saw that Sir Hugh had long lost interest—if, indeed, he had ever felt it—in his home affairs. From later remarks he made, it was evident that what remained of human enthusiasm in his vast frame was spent in petty speculations on the Stock Exchange. . . . It had been a strange interview.

"I have not said a word to Mamma," observed Anne. "I am afraid she will be troublesome. She has gone to spend the day at Ealing. But she doesn't matter!"

"Nothing matters," said Warre, "if you care for me."

And so—when that visit ended and he walked homewards—he laboured to convince himself. A momentary calm had settled on his spirit. He could think of Allegra with clear eyes and consider her coldness with a less implacable resentment. Was it worth his while to love so unresponsive a creature? Was not distance investing her with that convenient mist which alone makes it possible for any mortal to imagine extraordinary virtues in another? They were not friends in any accepted sense ; theirs had been an intimacy of silence, not words ; they had talked together very seldom. Was this because they could always understand each other without speaking? Because there was so subtle and close a bond between them that speech was needless? And whence came this sensation of their inseparability? Why, in spite of Allegra's manner, could he never think of her as some one apart—some one wholly divided from his life? He was like a man who hesitates between two religions—one, seeming good, promising much, possessing to all appearance every necessary nay, every covetable gift, and the other, mute, veiled, mysterious, inscrutable, yet with a power to draw the soul which neither casuistry, nor all the adverse evidence of the senses, nor accusations, nor mockery, nor scepticism can overcome.

"If I could only be cynical once more," said Warre, "only sneer with the rest, only laugh myself out of this enervating sentimentality. It must be a phase which we all have to pass through sooner or later. How long does it last?"

CHAPTER X

A Wedding

THE foolish young man did not allow either his relatives or friends an opportunity of opposing his engagement, but was married to Anne privately and by special licence just three weeks and a day from the time of their first meeting.

The morning was dull, and the sky was like the grey and lustreless marble of some underground tomb dimmed by the moisture of centuries. Simon drove to the church with Lord Wickenham, and they did not exchange a remark till the bridegroom discovered that he had forgotten his gloves. They halted at a small shop on the way and bought a pair. Warre found no difficulty in drawing them on; his hands were cold, stark.

"They are a devilish bad cut," observed his lordship.

"I must have told the fellow the wrong size," replied Simon.

"I suppose you have the ring?"

"Yes," said Warre, "I have the ring." He seemed to have been caught down into the world of inanimate nature—into the state of vitality without sense, without conscience, without pathos. He was neither glad nor sorry, agitated nor calm. And yet he glanced from time to time at his faithful friend, and remembered with surprise—as if it were a privilege long forgotten—that if he had been in trouble Wickenham would have helped him to bear it. It was just the look and the remembrance which a spirit released from mortality would give to the one he had loved during his days on earth, and who still lived, still thought this bodily frame a thing of consequence, the joys of this world worth striving for, its woe worth lamentation. Warre suspected, however, that Wickenham was distressed, and vaguely wished he could speak, wished he could say some word which—even though it could not bridge their estrangement—would take away its pain, its wretched mystery. Oh, to make him understand that he did not care—that he did not feel!

The carriage rolled on. Simon wondered whether it was the sound of the wheels which overwhelmed the murmuring in his brain. At intervals a pang of consciousness, keen and agonising, shot through the stupor. Formless, appalling, indescribable presentiments of despair, regret, and anguish beat their wings in the air, and uttered discordant cries, rapid, unintelligible warnings. Could he depart from his promise? Could he play the coward? Was it too late to turn back? And Anne waiting, perhaps already waiting at the church—happy, expectant. What right had he to spoil even a day of that fresh and innocent life because he had obeyed a desperate impulse, and asked her to marry him? Was not all the gift, all the loss, all the venture on her side? She loved him, too. It was a girl's love—pure, spontaneous, hardly conscious of its richness, ignorant of its own passion. How little he deserved it! Did all bridegrooms suffer from panic on their wedding morning? He decided that he was the base exception, and, much ashamed of a weakness which he would not for kingdoms have betrayed to Wickenham, he maintained the stern, imperturbable countenance which men, under the stress of emotion, assume in the presence of each other— an assumption which rarely fails to convince the male judgment, and which has never yet wholly deceived a woman.

As they approached their destination, Warre frowned. "I must get another coachman," he said. "Walton is too hard on the horses. He drives them at a frantic pace. Look at them now!"

"I don't see much the matter with 'em!" replied Wickenham.

Sarah Dane was already in the church. She sat near a young girl with black crape roses in her hat, who had wandered into the building out of curiosity. Two elderly men, who were fellow-clerks with Sir Hugh at the Bank, were also present. When they were not staring at the stained-glass windows within their sight, which were designed in memory of two Waterloo heroes and a Lord Mayor, they winked at each other. Lady Delaware was alone in a corner, wiping her eyes with a plain pocket-handkerchief, whilst a finer one, edged with old point lace, reposed on the ledge by her Prayer-Book, and under her red glass scent-bottle.

Warre and his friend walked down the aisle, and took their place at the choir rails, where, with their gaze fixed on the door, they waited without impatience or anxiety for the bride.

"Here she is!" said Wickenham quietly.

Warre could not look, but turned towards the

altar. The gold cross was bright; the flowers in the vases by its side seemed to be lilies. How could one mount such shining steps, or walk on such a polished floor? It was absurd. There was a church in Italy where he had always intended to be married, but it was not at all like this. He remembered the day when he saw it. Allegra was with him—an orange light fell on the ancient pillars till they glistened like some frost-bound forest of trees in a winter's sunset; it was not at all like this. The organist played ten bars of the *Wedding March*, but Lady Delaware begged him to cease, on account of her nerves.

When the ceremony was over they all went into the vestry. The elderly men made themselves agreeable to the bride; Sarah Dane held her skirt and wept; Lady Delaware showed by her expression that she considered Anne had thrown herself away; Sir Hugh fell into a benedictory mood and, mistaking the Registrar for one of Warre's obscure relatives, wished him a "God bless you!" He was greatly annoyed when he discovered his error. Anne cried when she signed her maiden name for the last time.

Simon did not see his wife until he found himself driving towards Portland Place with no Wickenham—but Anne—by his side. He wondered why he had ever thought her pretty, and what they usually talked about when they were alone, but nothing else passed through his mind.

Her hand stole into his. "I know!" she said, and smiled compassionately. "I know! You are nervous. Men hate these things."

CHAPTER XI

Two Men and Two Wives

ANNE wore a gown of dove-coloured cloth, and when she moved one caught glimpses of its white satin lining. Her bonnet was made of lisse and orange blossoms, and it rested lightly on her golden hair. No veil concealed her brilliantly pink cheeks.

"I really think," she said, "that Sarah might have ordered a new dress for my wedding. But it is very kind of her to give us a luncheon, because Algernon Dane is dreadfully mean about anything small. He will spend any amount of money on a big entertainment, because they can write about it in the papers; but when there are only one or two friends he gives them the claret he bought for Sarah, and the sort of *entrée* which is made with lots of carrots and gravy. I am looking forward to the dinners we shall give, darling. We can get all the best men if we only have good champagne, and pretty women, and all the hot things—*hot*. What is more terrible than a lukewarm joint? Algernon has no notion of living. Sarah said he did not come to the wedding because he had a headache. He went for a ride in the Row instead. Have you ever seen him on a horse? He looks like the last match left in a tray—the one which won't burn." An ecstatic smile flitted over her countenance. "Isn't it nice to think," she said, "that we are at last married for better or worse, and all that sort of thing? It is such a pretty idea, too, and so sensible. I love the Prayer-Book."

She was not prattling in her usual vein. She was not a woman of the soubrette type, and she was too grossly sentimental—too false in tone, as it were—to play the agreeable Rattle. She rarely used slang; she liked phrases long drawn out, the language of the pulpit and the romantic drama.

"I feel tired," she said to her husband, and seemed to droop. "I am not so happy as I thought I should be!"

Tears sprang into her eyes. And yet Warre could find nothing to say.

A few moments later the brougham stopped. They had reached Dane's mansion in Portland

Place. There was a crowd at the door—a wondering, muttering, ominously quiet crowd. What did it mean? Anne seized Simon's arm. There were dark stains on the pavement.

"Something is the matter," she cried. "I am sure that something awful has happened."

There was a man standing near the carriage, and he heard her words. "The gentleman was thrown from his horse just as he was turning the corner," he said.

Warre pushed him aside, and half carried Anne into the house. She shook like one stricken with the palsy; her face was ashen. "It is Algernon!" she kept repeating. "It is Algernon! I cannot believe it. And on my wedding morning!"

Algernon Dane lay on a rug in the hall. He was quite still; his eyes were closed; all his servants stood around him in brute amazement, watching, with curious horror, the blood which trickled from his mouth and nostrils. The housekeeper, who had been his mother's nurse, was wildly chafing his lifeless hands, sobbing out the pet names of his infancy, kissing the wounds on his forehead.

"Take me away! take me away!" screamed Anne. "Is he dead? is he dead? Take me away! Don't let me see him! don't let me look at him! Take me away!" She rushed blindly from side to side, and, in her impotent terror, beat the walls with her outstretched arms.

"He will kill me!" she screamed. "You don't understand. He will kill me. He will say that it was all my fault. You do not know him as I do. Don't let me see him!"

But Warre did not hear her. The sight of the injured man roused him from the trance which had held his soul for so many days. The awakening was so swift, so complete, so painful, that it seemed like the tearing away, by a strong hand, of some terrible blight which had overgrown his brain. He remained by Dane, who never recovered consciousness, and who died at last in Sarah's arms. She supported him tenderly, and lost all recollection of his unkindness, his brutality, his insulting neglect. She bowed herself over his dead and mangled body, and wept the bitterest tears of her sad life. She fancied it might have been different; that she had been to blame; that she had too often shown impatience. She had judged him too harshly. She and the old housekeeper clung to each other and murmured their fond account of his many virtues.

Anne had been taken to one of the ante-rooms,

where, losing all courage, she threw herself on the ground, rending her hair, tearing her cheeks, moaning, wailing, crying. When Warre came she grew more tranquil, her violence ceased. They left them alone together.

"Look at me!" she said, lifting her disfigured face; "look at me! Take me once more! Kiss me once more... and then... I will tell you..."

She fell on his neck and sobbed. "Would you say I was honest; would you say I was good, pure, faithful, all that even a bad man wishes a woman to be?"

"Dearest, how can you ask?"

Anne put her handkerchief to her mouth as though she would wipe the words from her lips even as she uttered them: "I was Dane's mistress. Dane was my lover."

"Never!" said Warre. "I will never believe it You do not know what you are saying!"

"For a whole year," said Anne, "for a whole year... and for money. Money! money! money! that was all I wanted! Money!"

"Never!" repeated Warre. "I say, this never was. It is a lie... a lie. It never was. You do not know what you are saying."

"I was Sarah's friend... she was very kind to me... I deceived her. And I deceived you."

Warre grasped her wrist. "Anne," he said, "this sounds too much like life. If it pleases you to act these parts . . . to make these hideous jokes . . . at such a time . . . keep them unsaid. This is too much like life. I cannot bear it."

She looked at him stupidly, with eyes that did not see. "It began," she said, "when I went to the Riviera with them last March. He gave me a fifty-pound note for my birthday, and told me not to tell any one . . . that only dishonourable women told other women what men gave them—what men said to them. I did not want to be dishonourable . . . and he was twenty years older than I . . . he knew the world so much better than I. . . . I suppose I was flattered . . . he was so rich . . . so many women ran after him. He always laughed when I said anything about trying to do right. . . it is not nice to be laughed at. He told me I was born for pleasure, not for edification . . . and he had so much common sense! I did not think I should ever get a husband. There did not seem to be any man who was so rich that he could afford to marry a poor girl! I was so poor . . . I saw nothing ahead . . . I did all he asked. He never treated me badly. He was generous. He loved me in his way! I suppose I have been very wicked . . . and yet . . . I am the only one who must suffer!"

Warre remained motionless.

"I have not injured any one," she continued. "Sarah did not love him. She would not grieve very much if she knew—except on my account. She would be disappointed in me . . . she is very fond of me. . . . As I said, Dane cared for me in his way, so I suppose I made him happy. As for me, I can deal with myself. But you . . ."

"I, too," said Simon. "I, too, can deal with myself. You said you were the only one who must suffer . . . the only one. You have not spoilt any life but your own! Think of that!"

She crept towards him on her knees, and, with tears streaming down her face, leant her head against his arm.

"Forgive me!" she sobbed, "forgive me! If you do not forgive me I shall kill myself. I don't deserve to live. Yet it was not my fault; he had a bad influence over me. And I am not cold like you; I am much more affectionate . . . I am more easily persuaded! Do you want me to go away from you for ever . . . never to see you again? Oh, say anything but that! You are my life—the very air I breathe—I cannot live without you! Since I have known you I have changed. And I cannot live without you! I cannot live without you! I love you! I love you! Do not send me away.

9

Let me be your drudge, your servant, your slave, only let me be near you! I will make you happy. Let me try; give me one chance. Oh, Simon, it was his fault! And I did not deceive you altogether; I said there was a man—like Algernon Dane—who wanted to marry me. Don't you remember? It wasn't possible to tell the whole truth; I could not betray him! A great many girls would not have been so candid. But I am naturally frank; I hate falsehoods. I need not have told you a word. But when I saw him dead . . . I wanted you to know . . . something made me speak. . . . You need not be so hard on me. You yourself told me that you were once in love with some woman. . . . I never reproached you. I don't suppose she was a saint."

A terrible expression of anguish, of despair, came into his face; she shrank away in fear. "I forbid you," he said, "I forbid you to speak of her!"

"Do you despise me?" asked Anne, crouching lower at his feet.

He drew a long sigh. "Come!" he said, at last. "Come! we must leave this house."

Anne watched him through her fingers. Was she not suffering a great deal of agony and remorse for nothing? He did not seem so angry. He did not seem to mind. If she had made such a confession to Dane he would have struck her, abused her shamefully, called her vile names. Simon was rather a fool.

"Say something kind to me," she whimpered. "Say you forgive me! Kiss me."

"Come!" said Warre again. "Come! we must leave this house."

"I don't want to pass *him* ... again!" said Anne.

She began to twist up her hair. Then she looked in the glass. "I look awful!" she exclaimed, and began to sob in self-pity.

"Come!" said Warre again.

As they passed through the hall they only saw the scullery-maid on her knees by a pail of water —only heard the swish of her scrubbing brush on the marble floor. Dane's body had been taken to his bedroom.

The little scullery-maid, with a white face and strong red arms, never ceased from her work, but continued the task of effacement.

One of the footmen—not observing Anne and Warre—called to her from the staircase.

"Chemicals is the only thing for that job!" said he.

CHAPTER XII

Disillusion

WARRE and his wife were to have gone to Lord Wickenham's villa at Weyborough to spend that perfect week which Heaven is said to lend the newly married. But Simon, on leaving Portland Place, ordered his coachman to drive back to Grosvenor Street. Anne thought him inconsiderate of her feelings. Surely she needed change of scene and fresh air after the terrible hours she had spent that day.

"I have always heard of the beautiful garden at Weyborough," she said. "I should like to see the famous apple orchard. I suppose you will go there to-morrow?"

"Why?" asked her husband.

"We must have a honeymoon," she replied. "What would people say if we remained in London? And Mamma would be indignant. She has all the old-fashioned ideas of etiquette. To go straight to Grosvenor Street! You are not nice to me. I do not want to be disagreeable, and I am sorry if you are vexed; but I must say that you are not nice to me! You have been very cold and very strange all day. Every one, I am sure, must have remarked it. Your married manner is not kind!"

It is only the cowardly and effeminate who are harsh towards women, who speak lightly of them, who effect a contempt for them, and treat them with contumely. Warre was at least heroic in one respect—he was, if anything, too lenient to the weak and fair, nay, even to the weak no longer, and perhaps, never fair. It was not in his nature to be severe with women; theirs was the harder part in the drama; theirs, the greater suffering; theirs, the heaviest punishment; theirs, the feebler frame. Anne's reproach cut him to the soul.

"Forgive me," he said; "God knows I do not mean to be unkind."

She threw herself back in the brougham and gave a sobbing sigh. She felt the satisfaction which comes of having been surprised into generous conduct, and she was even prepared to undergo a little sentimental suffering for her act of Quixotry. After all, she had confessed her fault; she had been foolishly honest; she had no secret now to conceal from Warre; no dread hung before her eyes. The future looked comfortable ; the dinner-parties and the interesting people could still be thought of. She had never claimed to be sinless, but if—from a sense of honour—she had concealed her intimacy with Sarah's husband, on one point, at least, she had not deceived Simon. She was— when the worst was said and the worst was done— a beautiful woman. A glance at the female occupants of every passing carriage was more than enough to remind her of this saving grace. No man in London had a prettier wife! And then she was a good companion ; she had superb health and excellent spirits. Other girls could talk on more intellectual subjects, but not one of those amusing chatterboxes had her perfect mouth, her dazzling teeth. Poor Algernon had been quick to appreciate her charms. Poor Algernon ! He had enthusiasm, he could admire beauty, he was intense. Simon worked too hard to be anything but dull. He was a dear, but dull; good-looking in a way, but too much like a stone Roman in a photograph of ruins ! Anne chafed under Warre's indifference ; he was unnatural. Why did he not ask a few sympathetic questions about Dane? He robbed confession of its legitimate pleasure, its highest recompense—the delight of stimulating curiosity and exciting interest —of appearing *far more wonderful than any book.*

When an unpleasant truth has once been admitted it often becomes not only the easiest, but the most enticing topic of conversation. Now that Warre knew the crude facts of Anne's story she longed to represent it in picturesque language, with all the romantic machinery of motives, remorse, and Divine intervention, against a background of ashen poverty. The weak mind is never weary of recounting its failures. An indolent spirit, which has once been stirred to the activity of transgressing in deed is never too languid to tell the history of its one lapse into the unhallowed toil of human sin.

"How is poor Sarah?" asked Anne timidly; "was she terribly upset?"

"She was very quiet," said Warre.

"Well," said Anne, "she is free at last! She can marry again, and, as she will have all Dane's money, she ought to get a titled husband! I am sure she deserves one. God orders all things for the best. If Algernon had lived he would only have grown more desperate, have committed more sins, have heaped upon himself a heavier load of iniquity, and a severer punishment hereafter. It was a merciful death!"

Warre listened in wonder.

"He was an extraordinary man," she added, "but he was deeply attached to me *in his own way*.

I tried to have a good influence over him, and I certainly kept him away from immoral women. Some of these creatures in society are so unscrupulous!"

"Anne!" Warre cried. "Anne!"

She studied him in surprise. Why was he so distressed? She could not understand him. And how ill he looked! How much better and more sensible if he had made a tremendous scene on the spot! Was he going to sulk and brood and say "*Anne*" in that awful way for ever? What a life! How could he expect her to care for him? He was not the only man in the world.

They crossed the threshold of their home in silence. The bride complained that she was hungry, adding that she thought she ought to force herself to eat. Why be more ill than necessary? Oh, she was so depressed! Simon ordered dinner to be served at once, and showed Anne the room which he had prepared as a surprise for her on their return from the honeymoon. It was furnished in olive-wood and old brocade; the style and decorations were in the early Italian manner and of formal beauty. Anne had the modern taste for the élaborate and meretricious; for that voluptuousness of environment, which supplies in substance what the enervated men and women of this century vainly strive to extract from their fatigued senses. She felt chilled by the austere luxury, but she saw at once that a large sum of money had been spent. So she clapped her hands, sat on all the chairs, looked long and happily in each mirror, blushed smiles at the chaste Cupids on the ceiling.

"And where does this lead?" she said, opening a door. "Darling, how dreary!" Simon was at heart ascetic. His bedroom was like a cell in a seminary; there was a small iron bedstead, a table, and a chair of varnished deal.

"When I go to sleep and when I wake," he said, "I like to see plain things."

"How funny you are!" said Anne. She would soon cure him of that affectation.

He went away alone to his study, entered it, and turned the key. For some moments he paced the floor; then he sat down at the table, with his face buried between his arms, suffering that agony of chagrin and disappointment which finds its earliest, and perhaps least poignant, expression in something which is more nearly physical than mental torment. His eyes were parched, thirsty, burning, for the tears he could not shed; the feverish hands he pressed to his aching temples gave them no ease; each breath he drew was like a three-edged knife; each sigh, a stab. And with all this there was a sense of suffocation, of blindness, of a powerlessness to move, of an infinite power to suffer. There was neither anger nor the desire for vengeance in the passion which convulsed him, but the feeling which is worse than either, because it is more enduring and more subtle, because when it has once entered into a heart it leaves its poison there for ever—the deep despair which is the counterfeit of resignation.

A voiceless cry beat on his silent lips like the lash of a whip.

"Anne! Anne! why did you do this thing? Why did you deceive me?"

The injustice of it all! What wrong had he committed to merit so humiliating, so cruel a disillusion? He had worked hard and faithfully all his life; the home he was now able to afford had been gained by many long and toilsome hours—toil, too, whilst others around him, of his own rank, played and fooled and trifled; had as much—much more than he—and as a matter of course, a birthright. Did he not work now as hard? Yes. Harder than ever. Surely he deserved a little happiness; he did not ask for much, nor did he hope for a long continuance of it, but he was only human. This new misery was beyond his strength. He could not bear it; could not, could not! All the small and great grievances, which, from his childhood to that latest day, had dismayed his spirit, fell on him with all their accumulated rancour. Pleasures are so much more difficult to remember than woes, and, while hours of happiness are dearer in their passage than in their recollection, hardship and suffering are resented more fiercely when they are overcome and outlived than at the time when the very necessity for their endurance produces a certain stupor. Simon felt again the pain of his frost-bitten hands and feet during those weary tramps to and fro West Kensington and the College; he remembered how he used to long for the warmth of the train, because his mother would only have one fire, and that in her own bedroom. He remembered the black, bleak mornings when he rose at a quarter to five, broke the ice in the tank for his bath, dressed in the dark, and sat, in a worn-out overcoat, writing Greek prose by the light of one tallow candle and an incomplete second-hand dictionary. He tasted again his dinners of thin mutton and stewed rhubarb; his luncheons off railway milk and halfpenny buns. Magnificent sustenance for an intellect doomed to travail for some ten hours a day! Would a brain so nourished be turned by a little love—a few earthly pleasures? It was hard! it was cruel! it was unfair!

A boy in the street passed under the window, and shouted, in strident tones, an obscene song.

"Here is the truth at last!" thought Simon. "He has defined life and love in four filthy, unspeakable lines!" As a rule he prescribed drugs and tonics for the cynical, merely to prove that a foredone soul is not to be exalted by quinine. But now he was not in the vein to offer mocking compliments to Materialism. There is a time when the possible Immortal in us will be no longer denied, no longer slighted, no longer called a stomach—to be calmed with roots and extracts, nourished on meats and milk. Warre's heart was breaking.

It was not Anne's sin which he found so hard to forgive; it was not for him to sit in judgment. But why had she deceived him? How could one who had so sinned look so innocent, show such a childish air, feign such an ignorance of evil? O hypocrite! Had he not seen her at church, lost in angelic self-forgetfulness, praying like some saint in a picture, her hands joined with the prettiest precision, her eyes mirroring the celestial light she lived by? O hypocrite! In his youth he had read deeply in the Scriptures, in sermons, in the writings of the Fathers; nowhere had he found such severity as Anne's—such biting wrath against the ungodly and unchaste. She could find no pardon for sins of the Flesh. She had made him feel so miserably unworthy of her; he had so feared to contaminate that virginal holiness. O hypocrite! First among stone-throwers! She seemed to him hideous, repulsive; in his sight all her beauty had perished; she was abominable. A woman who could assume chastity with such convincing effect should have small difficulty in its actual observance. Her conduct was inexcusable; she sinned—not from frailty, but for money. Had she not owned this? And yet—she was very susceptible to kindness. Words she had once used came back to him: "*What have I not done for companionship?*" Perhaps the horrible compact with Dane had been made from a false notion of gratitude on her part; young, inexperienced women—and sometimes those who were neither young nor inexperienced—were often foolishly polite, and suffered many scruples over the utterance of a negative. They thought it uncivil to say "No" to a benefactor. He knew of many such martyrs to delicacy. They had amused him—as one is amused at the pranks, the folly, the mischievous gambols of ridiculous pet animals; he could never treat their immorality seriously; they would frisk hereafter—small, black lambs among the heavenly host. They had nothing in common with the devil—they only suffered from an incomplete soul. But now he had married one. He did not find her so amusing, so artless, so innocuous as he had always held other men's wives of the same calibre to be. He saw Anne as he had met her first at Lord Wickenham's dinner: restlessly beautiful, eager for her dinner, eager for admiration; artificial in manner, singularly artless in so much that she said. Then at the boarding-house—that dirty, vulgar boarding-house—her peculiar manner with Dane and the painful tears which drowned her exit; the scene in the little conservatory—he still smelt the damp mould round the dying plants, still saw the faded paper of the Japanese lamps, still heard Anne's passionate sobbing, her bitter lament. And then that same evening, in this very room in which he now was, all that had been said, all that he himself had thought. She had sat where he sat at present. With a gesture of repugnance he stood up, pushed the chair far from him, and walked to the window.

The day had changed since morning, and now at sunset deep violet clouds, melting into grey and rose, were blown, like the petals of some strange flower, across the serene pale blue of the waning sky. It was a transient glory, and, even as Simon watched, the seeming petals were lost in apparent flames which licked up the horizon and consumed the sun, till by-and-by that, too, smouldered under the gathering vague and smoke of night.

"And this," thought Warre—"and this is like our hope—our love. A flower—a fire, and, after that, darkness!"

The injustice of it all! Was this anguish of mind a blessing or a reprimand; a life sentence or the stern discipline of a long but not unending day? It was his suspense, his uncertainty, it was his ignorance of the event which made the trial so wearisome and of a bitterness so irremediable. If he might only know why. If he could only be sure that it was not wanton cruelty, that he was not the sport of winds, the plaything of the gods, the devil's mouse. And yet how wildly he had scampered through this great crisis of his life; how wilfully he had disregarded the warnings of his own reason, the advice of his friend. How could he explain his own conduct? He was a stranger to himself. He remembered the saying of St. Paul:—

"*For the good that I would I do not: but the evil which I would not, that I do. Now, if I do that I would not, it is no more I that do it, but sin that dwelleth in me. For I delight in the law of God."*

Simon had heard many homilies on that frequented theme, and, for the first time in his life, he owned the benefit of listening patiently to a drowsy sermon. The sober sense and profound philosophy of the Church stuck fast. Warre had no dogmatic religion, but he had an instinctive and natural piety, which, though it did not show in his outward conduct or his ordinary conversation, nevertheless coloured his thoughts, and gave even his most rebellious moments that redeeming sweetness which makes all the difference between a vicious man and a man with many faults. He could not take refuge in the comfortable doctrine which teaches that one may be possessed of a demon for a night—or even for a few years—and still be held irresponsible for the fiend's vagaries. He sought for the ruling desire among the crowd of insurgent impulses which had swayed his moral being for the past six weeks. The admiration he had felt for Anne's beauty had died into a mere frigid acknowledgment before they had been engaged two days. He had never loved her; nor had he ever pretended to a deeper feeling than fondness. He had married her because he had believed so implicitly in her essential goodness—

her piety—both of which she had kept in the midst of temptation—without guardians, without love, without encouragement. And he was not easily deceived. He did not, as a rule, ask more of existence than it could give, or demand more from the nature of any other being than he found it was possible to bestow out of his own. He was not easily deceived. Once more and yet again he lived through every episode, every moment of his acquaintance with Anne. The wretched woman did not appear so false as—seen through the first blinding hurricane of disappointment—she had seemed. Cowardice and love of ease had been her undoing; hers was not the low cunning of a born adventuress, nor had she the self-control, the coldness, of an intentional traitor. She acted and spoke from her heart; unhappily, the heart was corrupt. But surely her remorse at least had been real, and the love she felt for himself was, whether hysterical, inconsequent, selfish, evanescent, or worthless, real. For that moment, at any rate, he was spared the pang of doubting the one poor gift of her affection. He would not—dared not doubt it. She cared for him, and he had married her. That was not base; not a wholly reprehensible motive. Perhaps there should have been more genuine devotion on his side. Ah! what was that other thought which he had swept from the argument—altogether out of the reckoning? He had not been true to himself—not true to Allegra. Away! away! all sophistry, all talk of settling down, of finding a convenient mother for one's unborn, but possible, family. He had abandoned hope of Allegra very soon; faint heart! His pride had been too easily wounded, his vanity too great; he had found it too hard to wait and be patient. He had expected to win a treasure for less than the asking—by a few kind remarks and a present. O fool! She was a shy little girl, not versed in the arts of courtship. He could remember—now it was too late—the many pretty signs she had given of a friendliness more than common. There is a tone of the voice, an unuttered and unutterable tenderness in the accent of true love, which no art can simulate and no discretion disguise. There is a glance which, even under the ice of an assumed indifference, or through the fiery tempest of quick anger, still wears the star of spring-time. There is a touch which is never so swift, so rough, so timid, or so unconsidered, but it manifests devotion. False affection may capture our vanity, but it never deceives our instinct; we may wish to be cared for, and, in the weakness of that strong desire, accept the protestation which our happiness or our self-esteem would believe in; but whoever took, with perfect honesty, venal, assumed, or base love for other than it was? Wickenham's words came back to him; the words of Wickenham, the frank, unequivocal man of the world and the flesh, the Pagan of our days. "If I had an ideal like yours, I should either stick to it or drop it altogether. If you consider it impossible, you are a fool to give it a second thought, and if it is possible, you are a coward if you accept anything less!" He had been a coward, had accepted the lesser thing. And found it the lesser, indeed!

His punishment was just!

"My God!" cried the unhappy young man. "I have accepted the laws of Nature and I have taught the laws of science, but yours is the only law I love. I have disobeyed it more than once. I have tried to forget it often. I have been unfaithful, and I am altogether a poor creature. But I worship what is good, and I hate what is vile; I have found no pleasure in disloyalty; I am wretched; my heart is like a gravestone; disappointment is the name of every fulfilled desire. Oh, where is peace to be found? We sin because we wish to be happy; the most dangerous temptations are those which promise heavenly happiness. I have tried all things except obedience. I am sorry! I am sorry!"

But if he could not escape the penalty of his wrongdoing, the lifelong infelicity, the undermining regret, the trembling endurance of a long-continuing present, the fearful expectation of a tardy future infinitely worse—promising nothing, threatening all things, save those to be prepared for and forestalled—if he could not escape this, he was free at least from the last shame, the one ineffaceable ignominy, the one irreparable disgrace. The woman who had the right to bear his name should never be his wife. He did not love her. One may love a sinner, an unfortunate, even the reckless sensualist, but not a hypocrite—not a being who could go to the altar with a lie on her face, on her lips, in her heart, acting the pure, young bride. Hypocrisy rises from a frozen hell; it blasts, it cuts our shivering charity, it beats and pinches like quick-fingered sleet, it enters with arrowy dart into our ice-bound kindness. And what was Anne's passion for him? Was it to be so much as named? What union, then, was possible between them? Where was the God who could bless it? Where was the

God who could call it a sacrament, an indissoluble bond?

He knelt down by the window, and, although his face was old from grief, there was that youth in his expression which neither years nor sorrow can rust or spoil. He wept, but without tears.

"Allegra," he whispered, "I have lost you beyond the shadow of a hope of a possibility. But you are mine, and I am yours; you are my beloved and my wife! The life divides us now, and some day death must take one of us away; but I will always love you, although I may never tell you so—although you can never know how dearly. And I will be faithful. I will not be faithless. Oh, my beloved, I will not be faithless!"

Was that a knock at the door? He listened. It was like an audible shivering of the wood, the tap of a woman's light fingers—fingers skilled in playing a musical instrument.

"I am here," said Simon.

"But you have locked the door," replied Anne.

He turned back the key.

She entered, bearing his small reading-lamp in one hand and holding up her train of heavy white satin with the other. The effect was theatrical, and she had intended it to be so;

the green shade gave an unearthly tint to her
face, lent it the tender melancholy she was not
only too tired then—but unable at any time
—to feel. But she had rare bodily beauty, rare
perfection of form and colouring; she was the
King's daughter among fair women; her feet
should have been clothed with the stars, her
raiment woven from the rainbow; a diadem of
suns would not have been too splendid for her
golden hair. Simon owned this.

She placed the lamp on the table. "I would
not let the man bring it," she said; "I want to
wait on you myself. I almost wish you had
no servants." Three of his unnecessary domestics,
however, had assisted at her toilette. She had
thought it wise to let them know at once that
she was accustomed to every attention; that they
would have to look well to their business. Her
gown was cut low, her neck and bodice glittered
with wedding presents, one of them a diamond
cross given by Lord Wickenham; the other, an
emerald moon, given by Dane. Warre's eye fell
on the trinket at once.

"Take that off!" he said sternly.

Anne coloured, and held her hand over the
ornament with a protective gesture.

"It was from Sarah as well," she faltered; "it

was from both of them. I can show you the card if you don't believe me!"

"Take it off!" repeated Simon.

"But it is sewn on," she said, "it is stitched to my dress. I never trust pins."

Warre took out his penknife. "What are you going to do?" cried Anne. "You will cut the lace! You will hurt me!"

"You know I will not hurt you," he said quietly.

He drew her towards the lamp, as though she had been a child, and, with a light touch, severed each minute thread which bound the brooch to her garment. She stirred impatiently, in the hope that he would either prick her or cut the satin; but his composure was marvellous, his dexterity, supreme. In less than two seconds —although it seemed to Anne much longer—he had disattached the bauble moon and thrown it, with cold contempt, out of the window.

"Don't cry!" he said. "I will give you something else."

"Every time I see Sarah she will wonder why I do not wear it. How awkward it will be! But when you buy the new one let me choose it myself. I am sick of emeralds; I should like a black pearl." Her good humour was restored; she would rather have had the emeralds as well as the pearls, but it was not a bad bargain. She put one hand on each of his shoulders and studied his haggard face with unfeigned concern. It would not take much worry, she thought, to make him a really plain man; he was always striking, distinguished, classic, but she did not want to see him lined and seamed by despairful meditation: that sort of thing did not attract her. And she honestly did not wish to fall in love with any one else: as Dane had so often and so wisely said, *why chop and change?*

"Darling," she said, with all the solicitude of a devoted wife, "my poor darling! You look tired to death. You need your dinner. And I am afraid you do not drink Burgundy! I must take care of you, precious!" She rubbed her soft cheeks against his; pressed languid kisses near his lips. She thought his coldness arose from fatigue, from exhaustion, and forgave it readily. Had she not partaken of wine and sweet cake and grapes, she, too, might have felt despondent . . . she, too, would have been unresponsive. The only affection she understood was that which rested on a tangible foundation; she liked the emphatic sanity of an after-dinner passion; there was one code of morals for Anne hungry, and another code for Anne well-fed; the scruples of Anne tired were not the scruples of Anne after a good night's rest.

She had sympathy for Simon. Her fond murmuring continued.

"Poor, little, disagreeable pet!" She pinched his ears, she stroked his nose, she kissed his chin. Warre's sense of humour was the only sense she stirred, but the laugh he stifled was not merry—it was like the grin which sometimes lives on the face of the dead who died in torment, bravely. He feared to meet her eyes lest she should see his extreme loathing of her caress and of her presence.

The ordeal of his relationship with Anne and its temptation was not the conflict between her allurement and his will, but that much more difficult encounter between a sensibility without strings, and a sensibility too highly strung—between a being of smiles and cries, and a being of iron and blood and tears.

"Anne," he said, "I was not prepared to hear what you told me this afternoon!"

"Oh! *that*," she murmured, and was at a loss for words.

"I will never refer to it," he said hurriedly; "it shall be a sealed subject between us, but I cannot forget it in a moment. Nothing can ever be the same to me again."

Anne flowered into a rosy pout, and, catching his coat-sleeve, pulled it softly to and fro.

"I said I was sorry! I said I was sorry! I said I was sorry!" she repeated with each gentle movement. "I said I was sorry! But you love me, don't you?"

Warre hesitated—not because he lacked an answer—but because he was so reluctant to wound even her vanity.

"You love me, don't you?" she asked again, never doubting.

The sternness of his reply did not betray the pain he suffered in its utterance.

"No," he said at last. "No! I do not love you."

Anne showed the incredulous air of some merciful goddess with a petulant but devoted worshipper, and made a mock effort to conceal an indulgent smile.

She dropped her eyelids, drew his arm more closely to her side.

"You *must* be very tired," she said.

It seemed to Warre that Anne's face had caught the infection of Dane's look; her girlish countenance bore the impress of his vice, like an obscene image printed on delicate wax. The air about her was an impure incense, heavy with the same noisomely sweet scent of civet which he had noticed about the head and clothing of Algernon Dane.

"What is the matter?" cried Anne.

Simon drew back, and his gaze was fixed on the little sharp knife which glittered. He made two attempts to speak, but could find no voice; then he picked up the knife, and slowly—as though it were the task prescribed him for eternity—closed it.

"Can't you see," he said, under his breath, "that if you do not leave me alone—if you do not go away—I shall kill you? And it will seem so right, so just. You are so evil a woman!"

He did not speak in any ecstasy of hatred. He was a man who had been driven too hard against the rude elements of reason; his heart lay shipwrecked on the barren soil by a dead sea. He saw no light; there was no day, and the atmosphere was foul with the odour of grave-things.

Anne slunk away like a courtesan who is at home with stealth, her footsteps noiseless, and insolent, low-laughing courage in her regard.

When Warre went up to his room that night Anne, who had been crouching for two hours by her door to listen for his footstep, cried out:

"Simon! Simon! I want to speak to you."

He entered.

She had thrown off her ivory satin gown, and it seemed in the dim light like a huge white serpent coiled up upon the floor. Anne wore a muslin jacket fastened closely to the throat, and with transparent sleeves. Her hair rolled in a dazzling torrent over her shoulders and below her waist. Her petticoat of shimmering satin, festooned with lace, just reached her naked ankles. She thrust her bare feet into a pair of Warre's old slippers. Her own small white ones, with their high heels and pearl-embroidered toes, were kicked, one, towards the window, and the other, by the wardrobe.

"I could not find my own bedroom slippers," she said angrily. "I was much too tired to unpack, and I will not trouble your servants. I found these in there," she pointed to his room. "They are too large and they fall off, and they are absurd. I am cold; I am miserable; I am worn-out. As for my dinner, I could not touch it. They brought it here, but I sent it away untasted. I forced myself to swallow some champagne, and I choked myself with a little chicken. I hate the housekeeper, and these maids who stare at me! You can send them away to-morrow. I will be treated with proper respect. What can they think? Do they know I am your wife? You will destroy my love for you. I know myself well, and it is not in me to care for a man with a sulky, selfish, brutal disposition. I am sorry, darling, to speak so plainly, but now we are married it is not worth while to disguise our true characters and our real feelings. Between husband and wife there should be perfect sincerity —absolute confidence. I have just been reading Jeremy Taylor's sermon on *The Marriage Ring*, which poor mamma put in my dressing-bag. She always said that happiness could not be found with a husband who had no deep-rooted religious belief. Her words were true."

"Anne," said Warre, "we have both made a terrible mistake. I regard our marriage as a legal contract, which does small honour to either of us— nothing more. It is for me now to speak plainly. I am sorry if I appear harsh. But if I minced words now it would only lead to worse and more hideous trouble. You are not my wife—you never will be my wife. You have the right to bear my name——"

She tittered. "It is not particularly distinguished," she said. "What did you tell me your poor father was? A coachman? a carpenter? a tinker? a tailor? a candle-stick maker?"

"He was an honest man," said Simon. "He spoke truth all his days, and he lived cleanly."

"I have never met any one who had the pleasure of his acquaintance," replied Anne, with heaving breast. "I daresay, however, he was a highly respectable person. What does it matter to me what he was? I did not marry you for your honest father, but for your money!"

At this last cruel taunt, sudden, scalding, uncontrollable tears broke through Warre's sunken eyes.

"You shall have my money," he said quietly. "I will earn all I can. In case anything should happen to me, I insured my life yesterday. And if I merely fall ill, I have settled a sufficient sum on you to keep you at least in comfort."

But Anne had now huddled herself in a chair, and was crying bitterly. She loved Simon after her feline fashion. The betrayal of her avarice was a self-revelation which, before it penetrated Warre, first glinted sharply—not without damage—against the artificial ideal she had formed of her own character. It had pleased her to regard her marriage as one of pure and disinterested affection. The astonishing power of self-deception which she had inherited from Lady Delaware had become, from the circumstances of her life, a malady of the mind. And when she caught glimpses of her true self, she suffered, just as those who are afflicted with madness suffer, when the sound of some long-forgotten tune calls up a painful and evasive half-remembrance of serener days.

"Oh, I never meant to say that!" sobbed Anne. "I never meant to say that. Why did you make me lose my temper? I told you I had a bad one. This day will kill me!"

She looked up to implore his pity, his forgiveness, but he had gone.

"Simon!" she called, "Simon!"

She flung herself against his door; listened, and there was no sound; cried out his name once more, and there was no answer. He was not there. He had returned to his study. She knew that it would be useless to follow him. And she was so tired.

For some moments she stumbled blindly to and fro the two rooms; then she picked up her gown to fold it away. But before she reached the wardrobe she let it fall again on the floor. She went to her box and took out a glove case and a feather fan. She shook out the fan, caressed the ostrich tips, counted the gloves, put them back. She spent ten minutes looking for her dressing-slippers of swansdown and white silk, and found them, at last, where she had thrown them without knowing it—on the bed. Then she walked once more to Simon's room, tapped, and went in. It was still empty. She laid his old shoes where she had found them—under the deal table—and dropped her tearful handkerchief by her side, shedding innumerable fresh tears the while.

Alas! Why is there no Eden for such Eves? Why is it that only God is good enough and the devil bad enough to be safe in their company?

She sobbed herself to sleep on the floor. Simon spent the night in his study.

CHAPTER XIII

Reality

AT sunrise Anne awoke. Her limbs ached, and she felt cold. She returned, hoping that she had caught a severe chill, to her own room, and, with a sufficiently genuine wish that she might die before the evening, undressed, nestled in the bed, and sank into a deep but troubled slumber.

When she opened her eyes again it was ten o'clock, and Simon was standing by her side. The fatigue and violent emotions of the day before had impaired, for the time, her excessive prettiness. She was now an ordinary, tired woman, with listless tresses, uncertain features, dull cheeks, and a pale mouth. She had twisted one lock of her hair into a curling-pin which gave that note of the grotesque to her appearance so common, and often so fatal, in domestic tragedy. But in all the pride of her beauty, her costly gowns, her theatrical posings and vapourings, she had never touched Simon's heart so nearly as she did at that worst, critical moment when all her personal charms were under eclipse. There is a silent eloquence about the human and commonplace which is more dangerous to a kind and honest nature than any passionate appeal, any elaborate assault on the senses, any armament of finery, civet-sweet smiles, or languishments in lace.

Anne made as though she would timidly offer him her hand, but drew it suddenly back.

"I know," she sighed, "that you would not take it!"

He took them both, held them in both his own, then let them go again, as though they were little wild birds he had tried to love into docility.

"I have been thinking over what you said about going away," he began, "and, although I cannot go to Weyborough, I will take you anywhere else. Paris might amuse you."

She shook her head.

"Nothing can ever amuse me again," she said. "Nothing can ever be the same to me again!"

True to her mimetic instinct, she had borrowed, without knowing it, Simon's own words of the night before—Simon's own manner in saying them. Warre's anguish had been so real and so profound that even Anne's imitation of it was moving, and, as he himself did not perceive that it was but an apish copy of his own pain, it was harder for him to see this mere reflection of adversity in his miserable companion than to suffer the original grief.

The offending coquetry in Anne had been so drenched by her tears, that every womanly wile, every instinct of cajolery she possessed, was drooping and half dead. She made no effort to attract Warre or to excite his compassion, but lay there—a sexless creature, with quivering lips and weary face.

Unconsciously he stooped and kissed the sharp frown from her forehead; it was the first time he had kissed her since their marriage.

"Poor little girl!" he said.

Anne gave a drowsy sigh, and, with childish unconcern, turned herself toward the wall and fell asleep again. He folded the blankets more closely round her shoulders and drew the window-curtains nearer, lest the light should tease her eyes.

Then he went away.

It seemed to him that it might yet be possible for them to find some happiness together . . . if not as husband and wife, at least as friends. He had always mocked with the rest of the world at the notion of any mere comradeship between a man and a woman. In all such relations there was always one, at any rate, whose gaiety walked in sackcloth, whose admitted devotion was a heart-breaking privilege. Wickenham, he remembered, was the fierce opponent of every falsely sentimental theory on the subject of so-called Platonics.

"Why don't the fools begin by reading their Plato?" he would say. "Let 'em study the *Phædrus*. It's a complete give-away of the whole fraud. And devilish well-written too. The old scoundrel!"

But Wickenham did not know all things, nor Plato all things!

That same afternoon Simon and Anne started on their strange honeymoon. She did not look pretty, and her eyes were like forget-me-nots after an unseasonable fall of snow. She was still so exhausted that she slept on the way to Dover.

When they reached the Channel, Warre opened the window.

The clouds looked as though a mountainous sea had been caught up into the sky and was tossing its froth over the steely plains of night. The wind sang a strange song. Anne woke up, and trilled a little scale in response. Simon had not heard her sing before; her voice was like a fairy flute. He had never guessed its sweetness.

The two sat on the deck of the steamer, and, when Anne was not dozing, she laughed at the huge green waves, the absurd little boat, and her own discomfort.

Who would not have been charmed by such innocent and unusual amiability?

Poor little girl!

She talked a little, and told him three small, wholly superfluous lies—one, about the price of her hat; another, about her former visits to Paris (she had been there but once, and for one day only); and the last, about the number of governesses who had assisted at her education. The first taxed his credulity; the second he knew was an untruth; and the third he had every reason to doubt.

Why could she not be honest?

The pity of it! And the hopelessness! The shame of it! And the mystery!

How could a woman be so eminently lovable in many ways and yet be so treacherous? Look so gracious and be so abject? Lies, he thought to himself, were mainly told for two causes—vanity and cowardice. Poor Anne often lied merely to make conversation. The truth so rarely occurred to her.

At Calais, she went ashore and climbed into the train, holding her skirts, apparently by accident, well above her ankles. The male passengers surveyed them with admiration; she had brushed against one who had a heavy moustache and was handsome. They had apologised to each other. She had thought his smile charming.

"Never do that again," said Warre, when they were seated.

"What?" she asked, with a splendid blush.

"It is so vulgar," he replied.

"How could I help it?" she said. "Besides, I did nothing. I cannot drag these good clothes through the mud, and if I tread on some unfortunate person's toe (was it a man or a woman? I really could not see, for I was so afraid lest I should lose you) if I tread on some poor creature's toe, I must at least beg his pardon. You are unreasonable, darling!"

Anne thought, however, that his remark arose from marital jealousy, and she was, therefore, too flattered to feel any resentment. And was it not rather clever of him to have seen through her trick? He was not such a simpleton, after all! Women respect a man whom they cannot deceive, but only when he has the generosity to warn them of his discernment. It is fatal to feign a belief in their fooling, to beguile the beguiler, and then, after a period of mutual deception, to analyse, with cynical accuracy, each enchanting falsehood, every distracting gesture.

Anne was impressed by the discovery that Warre would not stand any nonsense.

She took a little worn book out of her ulster pocket and began to read her night prayers. She also asked herself the various and searching questions given for the examination of one's conscience. This duty finished, she prayed for Simon's conversion to the Anglican Church, and at last fell asleep, wondering whether he had forgotten the black pearl and whether her gowns would look fashionable in Paris.

CHAPTER XIV

More Realities

THE hotel to which Warre had telegraphed for rooms was a quiet one, and Anne's heart sank at its appearance until she learned that it was not only famous for its *cuisine* but more expensive than the Continental.

Their salon was regal with red damask, a large glass chandelier, marble tables with gilt legs, and several mirrors.

"It reminds me of one of the ante-rooms in Buckingham Palace," observed Anne, in a loud tone, "or am I thinking of Balmoral?"

The manager, who had conducted them to the apartment, bowed, and for the wear and tear to his backbone mentally added five francs a day to their bill.

When the man had gone, she remembered that Simon knew she had never been to Scotland.

"You see so many photographs of Balmoral and

all these places," she explained, "they become so familiar to you—that—you—seem to have spent years in them."

She saw his mouth twitch, and she threw her arms round his neck.

"I am a dreadful little snob, and I know it," she said. "But snobs get the best attendance, and the nicest rooms, and the most comfortable chairs and all that kind of thing wherever they go. And everybody wants to know them and everybody asks who they are. You are so quiet that I wonder how on earth you get on in your profession. Geniuses are always disappointing in their air! If I had your gifts, I should let people know it by my manner."

Warre heard the voice of Algernon Dane in each word she uttered. Would he ever grow accustomed to it? He changed the subject by asking her what she would like for her breakfast and when she wished to have it. It was then about two o'clock in the morning. She expressed an appetite for omelette, coffee, and rolls, which were to be served at nine. He did not ring for the waiter, but left Anne to give the order himself at the office.

When he returned, he found the door, not by its number, but by a pair of little boots on the mat.

They were pretty, and gleamed with patent leather cut in patterns. He had seen them at Calais; so had the porters; so had all the male passengers; so had the good-looking man with a heavy moustache. Warre passed them, and entered his own desolate room hand-in-hand with despair.

At breakfast that morning Anne was in the highest spirits. She talked French to the waiter, and encouraged him to correct her accent. To please him, too, she abused English cooking, and wondered why one could not get a decent omelette, or coffee one could drink, out of France.

The day was superb, and the air was so blue that one seemed to be looking at the whole world through a transparent turquoise. The sound of the wheels and horses in the street was lighter, quicker, merrier, pitched in a higher key than the solid, thunderous rumble of London traffic. Anne liked the bells which jingled and tinkled, and flung back the windows to hear them more distinctly. The sun fell on Simon's head. Anne knew that many men were extraordinarily sensitive on the subject of baldness.

"Darling," she said kindly, "you work too hard. Your hair is getting thin." She had not yet arranged her own, and, as it was only caught up by one pin, she made a sly movement and shook it free.

Oh, how tired he was of that golden mane!

"I wish," he said drily, "you could manage to keep it tidy. It looks all right for about ten minutes, and then it tumbles down."

They each laughed a little, and pretended to be joking. But they did not deceive themselves or each other.

"I suppose you know a number of nice people here?" said Anne presently. "You must call on the Cavernakes at once." Lord Cavernake was a distant connection of Warre's, and lived, with his wife, in Paris. "And then," she continued, "I want to meet some of the French nobility, and some of the best artistic set. I do not care about sight-seeing. One can run through the Louvre in a morning. But, before we do anything, you must hire a proper carriage. Two horses, of course."

"We can only stop here a week," said Warre, "because they want me at the hospital. It is not worth while beginning the tedious business of paying calls and dining out. We ought to be able to amuse ourselves by driving, and going to the theatres, and seeing what is to be seen."

"Just like one of poor Papa's clerks on his honeymoon!" said Anne. "I remember a dreadful little man called Salisbury, who married a governess, and they stopped two days at the Grand Hôtel—not knowing it was considered rather disreputable. And they used to hire a *fiacre* for three hours every day. They saw everything in the guide-book, and always dined at a Duval. They said they had never tasted such excellent chicken for the money, but the salad gave them indigestion. He called one Sunday afternoon and told us all about it. Mamma was civil to them because she is naturally kind, and also because Salisbury's father is in a wine-merchant's, somewhere in the City, and he can get us the best Burgundy at half-a-crown less than the Store price. Algernon Dane tasted it, and he said it was every bit as good—if not better—than some he bought at Lord Winterbourne's sale at one hundred and forty-five shillings the dozen. . . . But why not call on the Cavernakes? Are you ashamed of me? Who was Lady Cavernake? Her father was a curate at Ealing. Mamma has seen him giving blankets to old women. And he was the sort of man who preached in a black gown!"

She suddenly felt ashamed.

"I suppose," she said at last, "that an empress would get common and say vulgar things if she lived long in a boarding-house. I wasn't born to be a snob, dear, but everything has been against me. I have not had any chance. I wonder that I am as refined as I am!"

She went into her bedroom, and he feared she was going to cry. But she had discovered that it was only necessary to hint at the boarding-house to rouse his compassion. So she spared herself the fatigue of weeping, and, instead, dressed in her prettiest clothes.

Anne's confidence in her beauty was so great, and her belief in Simon's infatuation so complete, that, in spite of his indifference (which she easily attributed to fatigue and jealousy), she felt quite sure that his absolute subjection would mean, at most, a few days' struggle. And, sure of her ultimate victory, she enjoyed the prospect of battle.

"He adores me!" she said, as she shed penitence on her cheek with a powder-puff. "He worships me!" she said again, as she brushed her eye-lashes with rose-water. She always found rose-water a convenient and painless substitute for tears. She was sorry that she made that severe remark about his hair, but it was only fair to warn him that she was fastidious . . . indeed, particular. Besides, it was a great mistake to be grateful to any man. The gratitude ought to be on *his* side. And with her looks! Simon had the best of it, decidedly.

For the rest of the day they were studiously polite. In the afternoon they drove in the Bois, and in the evening they went to the Français. Warre promised her, as they returned, that he would buy her the black pearl on the morrow. She had to lean out of the carriage window to hide her smile of triumph. Men were such simple creatures! Just like children.

As his tone grew kinder, her manner became more demure. She drew up in the corner of the carriage, and begged his pardon, when, the wheels sinking suddenly in a tram line, she was thrown against his arm.

The comedy had been *Francillon*. Anne could find no excuse for the heroine's conduct, but she thought the husband made a sinful mistake in neglecting her. Like most people who trifle with life and its responsibilities, she took all purely artificial things in terrible earnest. Anne would spend hours discussing the wickedness or virtue of imaginary characters in a play or in a romance, and dismiss the events of her own existence in one sleepy " Forgive us our trespasses."

A well-cooked dinner, champagne, the theatre, and a knowledge that her appearance had created a sensation—every opera-glass in the building had been directed at their box—all these circumstances gave her an efflorescent good-humour. She called Warre's attention to the moon, and was greatly touched by an old woman whom she saw in the street and who she feared was hungry.

"What a pity," she exclaimed, "that the man is driving so fast, or you might give her half-a-franc. I left my own purse at home. But how thankful we ought to be, darling, that we are not called upon to bear such cruel trials to our faith. Poor creature! Yet I daresay, if we knew her life, we should find that she had many compensations even for this apparently insupportable suffering!"

While Simon read his letters in their salon at the hotel, she stood by the window, gazing up at the stars; then, not offering to kiss him good-night, went quietly away to her room—to take off her hat, as she said. But she did not return.

Warre smoked for half an hour, expecting her reappearance (probably in one more new gown, and with her hair down her back), and not asking himself whether he should be glad or sorry if she came.

Other men that evening had eyed him with envy.

Why was it so impossible to love her? The life they were leading could not continue. One day of sham marriage had convinced him of his folly. It was not only morbid, unwholesome, and insane, but profoundly ridiculous. He never thought of Allegra now. It would have been unfair to both women. Like all men in a false position, he was full of sophistries. He called himself a married celibate, and laughed at the droll paradox. Anne was certainly beautiful, and she was not more mercenary than others. He believed she was fond of him, in spite of her taunt about his money, and in much the same mock-generous strain in which he had wished her benefits on the first evening of their acquaintance, he began to wonder how he could make her happy. Was it not his duty to try and exert a good influence over her character?

This thought brought his spirit such consolation and his mind such ease that, by-and-by, when he went to bed, he slept for ten hours without stirring.

The next morning Anne was very silent. She gave long sighs and little forced smiles. They visited the Louvre and Notre-Dame. She was shocked by some of the works of art, and, in Notre-Dame, prayed for some time. They were obliged to return to the hotel to have the dust brushed from her gown, for, rejecting a *prie-dieu*, she had knelt on the pavement. At luncheon she ordered champagne. She was really not strong enough, she said, to be devout. And yet, for example's sake, she always made it a rule to pray when she entered a church. After the champagne, she had some yellow Chartreuse. Then she felt sufficiently restored to make a fresh toilette, and suggest a visit to the Madeleine. She arrayed herself in the cloth gown she had been married in, and a large hat adorned with superb plumes. It was an exact copy of one worn by a popular actress in the part of a virtuous courtesan. Warre remarked that the bonnet was more becoming.

But Anne was looking handsome, dashing, brilliant, and she knew it. The hat was not changed, and, as they walked through the street, every passer-by turned to look after them. No one supposed for an instant that she was the wife of her sad Englishman; the men thought him fortunate but indiscreetly proud of his discovery; the women exchanged glances, and the children stopped playing.

On their way to the church they halted at a book-shop, where she chose half a score of French novels. She knew the language well enough to understand the untranslatable. Warre did not approve of her selection, but he did not like to seem a martinet; she said, too, that she read certain authors solely for their descriptions of scenery. When they reached the Madeleine she was too tired to enter, but as they had sent their carriage there to wait for them, they stepped into this and drove off to the Bois. Yet the drive gave her no pleasure, because their victoria and pair was only a hired one. Whenever a block occurred, she would say, in a loud voice to be overheard by those who were sitting in carriages or standing on the footpath near them:

"What a pity we did not bring Walton and the brougham and the dear horses with us! They would have enjoyed this so much!"

Warre was indiscreet enough to point out the Cavernakes' landau, which, containing the governess and the eldest girl, happened to roll past.

"What a *very* plain child!" said Anne. But she was horribly depressed. The fine carriage and the coronet on its panels had excited her envy. Why was she not a peeress? What was a genius after all, no matter how eminent in his profession? And a curate's daughter had caught Lord Cavernake. How had the little snob managed it; and without a penny, too, or grand connections? Her name was Eliza Lesser, and her grandfather had been in trade.

"Why did he marry her?" she asked Simon,

when they got home. She had been brooding in silence over the subject all the way there.

"He loves her," he replied, "he is devoted to her. She is the sweetest creature in the world. All men do not marry for money."

"I know that!" said Anne, with a sudden impulse of affection. "I know that, darling! Didn't you take poor little poverty-stricken me? But you do not love me as you used. You will not give me any opportunity to show my gratitude. You are so cold and stern. Never mind! never mind! I shall always love you just the same, no matter what happens. But oh! if I had only been brought up like Lady Cavernake in some quiet little home in the country . . . hearing only good things and meeting only good people!"

She rushed into her room and wept hysterically. Simon found himself a mean brute, and went out for a walk. How was all this going to end?

When he had gone, Anne read the *Morning Post*, which her mother had sent her from London. The fashionable news made her wretched. How she would have enjoyed that house-party at the Duke of Gaunt's. That hideous, badly dressed, imperfectly washed Elizabeth Hastings went everywhere. And why? Merely because she had three thousand a year. Then the dinner at Moreton

House. Did Simon know the Moretons? They knew every one. But fancy their inviting the Winnipegs to meet a Royal personage! Who were the Winnipegs? They were not at all well off, and never entertained. Some people had such luck. Oh dear! She was sick with discontent.

That night she would not dine in the restaurant of the hotel as usual, but, complaining of headache, ordered the dinner to be served in their sitting-room. It was stupid, yet she imagined that it was the sort of dull thing Lady Cavernake would like and men would think her *sweet* for liking.

"The last time I was in Paris," said Warre, quite innocently, "the Cavernakes were only here on a visit—they lived in Rome at that time—and we all stopped together at this hotel. We had that little table near the window."

"Which little table?" asked Anne.

"The one in the restaurant downstairs," said Warre, "where the fat man with the three thin daughters sat last night. It was very jolly!"

Anne pushed away her plate. Simon began to *get on her nerves.* She hated everything and everybody. Oh, to be dead! But, in the meantime, more champagne. Dane had trained her to believe in the splendid efficacy of this tonic, and to regard any sober mood as *low spirits,* perilous to her beauty, her health, and her happiness. Warre, to restrain her, drank the greater part of the bottle himself. She ordered another. By the time they had reached the dessert she looked like a young Bacchante. Youth was still in her favour. It was only in rare moments and sidelights that the hard lines and coarse flush of the future threw their ugly forecast on her face.

Simon was by nature extremely temperate; but idleness, the desire to escape from his own despair and Anne's companionship were already beginning to have a demoralising effect on his mind. Why not accept the inevitable? Why not make the best of the inevitable? Why not make the best of an inevitable which was really not unpleasant from several points of view—the robust, Pagan point of view, more especially? The thought was fast becoming more elaborate. Words develop strangely; the root may be a meagre thing, barren, dry, yet it will yield a whole system of ethics.

Anne's conversation took a poetic strain, and she used all the pretty phrases she could remember from the songs she had learnt—many of them the compositions of Elizabeth Barrett Browning and Adelaide Proctor and Shelley. Dane had besmirched every one with his impure innuendoes, for he discovered vice even among the flowers, but what little womanly sentiment the girl possessed still hovered over certain tender lines which no foul explanation could make entirely hideous. She knew now that Simon was not to be won by the coarse blandishments which flattered the profound vulgarity and depraved instincts of Algernon Dane. It had been the one mental pleasure in his career to pour vile knowledge into her young, impressionable mind. He had tried the same system with Sarah; she had withered under it at first, hiding herself away from the sight of all creatures, but she had lived her childhood among pure women and chivalrous men; she was older, and stronger, and wiser than Anne; she had strong principles, and a sound, commonplace temperament. She had only been troubled for a year or two.

Anne's character, however, had received its permanent tinge. Her innocence was lost in the blackness of darkness for ever. Yet she was relieved to find that Simon was different, and to suspect that even all worldly men—those who *knew how to enjoy life*—had not the tastes of her destroyer. The unfortunate woman watched Warre timidly, and, at last, with tears in her wistful eyes, said:

"Why didn't I meet you first?"

It was too pitiful. She continued:

"I will never ask you to forgive me, dearest.

But some day, when I am old, and tired, and sad, and you think I have suffered enough, perhaps you will tell me that I am forgiven. You are the only one in the world who has ever been kind to me, dear. Dane never loved me at all. Days when I didn't look my best he was always rude and neglectful. And now, when I think that I have lost your affection for ever . . . that it will never be mine again . . . never, never, never again—I wake up in the night and I fancy that the room is my grave, and I draw the sheet over my face and say: 'Hide me now I am dead. No one cared for me while I lived, and in death I am all alone. But I am misery's love; misery and I are buried together. Let the worms eat misery first!'"

At this horrid thought she grew pale and cowered before the terrors of her own imagination, a trembling, haunted, hunted soul.

She seized her liqueur-glass and drowned a scream with its contents.

Then she laughed.

"My God! We must live while we live. If you turn back from going to the devil, it is as bad as turning back from the way to heaven. For then you don't arrive anywhere. The good ones won't have you, and you bore the bad ones. As you begin, you must end. That is only common-sense."

She stood up and went towards the door.

"I am going out into the street, where I belong," she said; "there I shall find a few friends; they will be kind to me. But I must not put it off too late—till I have lost my looks. Thank God, I am pretty. . . . They will be very kind to me; they won't make me feel so beastly miserable!"

Nevertheless, she turned back, and, with a wild cry, flung herself on Warre's breast. "Save me from myself! Save me from these other men! Oh, Simon, save me from these other men! I know them. Dane wasn't the only one. But the others were for love; one had to marry a rich girl, and the other was already married to a dreadful widow with money. I have been so unlucky. I no sooner quarrelled with one bad lot than I met another! Oh, Simon, you must save me from myself!"

This confession did not surprise him. After the first disillusion, science and sentiment had wrestled in his soul for her character, and, although he had never owned the result in clear thoughts, Anne herself had now said it for him. He bowed to the appalling declaration. She was a wanton.

"Why make these terrible scenes?" he said quietly; "why refer to these things which I want you to forget? Finish your coffee, and then I will take you out. This room is too close!"

But women like Anne only live in *scenes*, and she gew sullen, as she usually did when Warre showed no disposition to play his part in her riotous drama.

"I shall say what I please!" she answered. "I hate your supercilious airs and your quiet way. Why can't you speak out?"

She took up her cup, and, pretending to aim at Warre, dashed it on the ground. She always had a certain cunning control over her very abandonment.

"I told you I had a temper! Now you can see it for yourself!"

The saucer and the fruit-plate were hurled next. One missed his face by an inch.

"And now," she shouted, "I hope you are satisfied. You have spoilt my whole evening! My God, you would try the patience of a saint! *Don't make these scenes!*"

She mimicked his voice, and made diabolical grimaces till she caught sight of herself in the mirror. Then she shrieked with fright.

But her tongue soon recovered its abuse, and for the next half hour, Warre listened to threats, complaints, oaths, and obscenities. Yet there was something so wild and irresponsible about the afflicted soul that he could not feel anger. She only aroused the immense and speechless pity he always suffered for those blighting and blighted creatures called hysterical. His soul wept as he watched her.

Anne went at last to her room, but not until she had sobbed her remorse on Warre's breast, imploring his forgiveness, and suggesting that he still loved her.

"Kiss me! Say you love me a little, darling! I don't know what I have been saying, but I never meant a word of it. Precious! don't look so depressed; it depresses *me*. Smile, dearest. All women are unladylike when they get in a temper; they remember all the things men have said to them! Darling, I want you to smile."

When she had gone, he went out into the air. He chose a dark street, and no man saw the tears he shed, alone, in the night of that gay city.

The next morning Warre received a telegram from London summoning him to a consultation. When Anne heard that the patient was Mr. Samuel Wenslow, the great auctioneer, she was not only willing but anxious to return at once.

"You can make him pay well for the inconvenience and disappointment," she said. "He is as rich as Crœsus. And how well he used to dress Mrs. Bolingbroke! I have seen them at the Savoy, but he always took his wife and Bolingbroke as well. I never saw a man so careful! If he went into the country for a Sunday, Bolingbroke and the little boy had to go too. And now the poor old thing has got paralysis. You must cure him, dear, for Mrs. Bolingbroke's sake. She is a good little woman with a rather attractive squint. And so kind to the poor!"

CHAPTER XV

Plain Facts

ANNE seemed very happy to find herself once more in her Italian boudoir, and every morning, before she fatigued her voice by giving orders to the housekeeper, would sing for two hours or so at the Steinway piano. Warre, in his study underneath, seeing patients or writing his new book on Nervous Disease, used to wince at the sound of the slow scales and quick arpeggios, but he did not like to complain of her innocent pleasures. One afternoon she was seized with a whim to be economical, and engaged a woman to come with a sewing machine, which, while he laboured to compose a lecture for the Royal Institution, rumbled over his head from three till seven. At dinner Anne showed him four yards of massacred velvet, representing two guineas. The wretched sempstress had a sick husband and three children with the croup! It was a charity *to go out of one's way* to find work for the poor soul!

But Anne, in her manner, had now become very quiet and most demure. She no longer protested her love, but, like a child, used to kiss Warre good-night and good-morning on the cheek. In the afternoons she drove out with Sarah Dane, who, glad of distraction, accompanied her into shops, and admired her wonderful taste in selecting furniture for the drawing-room. Anne postponed all visits and visitors, returned no calls, and discouraged those who would pay them, because, as she said, her home was not in order. Sometimes, after dinner, she would read aloud to Simon or embroider crooked initials on some handkerchiefs which she had purchased at a sale, for his birthday. She was always very thrifty when she bought presents.

Her dresses now were in delicate shades of heliotrope, peach, and twilight blue — simple eighteen-guinea gowns, which dear, clever Simon could earn in a morning, without trouble. He had only to sit in his study and write prescriptions. What a talent!

She never asked to be taken to the theatre, and, when Sarah invited them to dine with her, very quietly, to meet her trustees (handsome

Colonel Dane of the Guards, and that great man of the Turf, Sir George Durham), Anne grew rather flurried, and said for some reason she did not care to see strangers. Sarah, who was never at a loss for the conventional explanation of any mystery, thought she understood the young bride's diffidence, but was too shy and reserved a woman to do more, in consequence, than treat her friend with a grotesque tenderness. Mrs. Warre was not to be thwarted or contradicted, and, when their shopping reached the second floor of any establishment, Sarah would ascend the staircase first, to see whether it would be worth Anne's while to mount it also. She ordered flowers and fruit to be sent to Grosvenor Street daily from her country house in Essex, and, as she was extremely dexterous at lace-making and fine needlework, she made up a wonderful basket, which she would hide, with a blush, when she heard Anne's footstep. Once, when she found her friend rather downcast, she said, with guileless cunning:

"Your figure looks extremely well, dear, in that blue cloth!"

"Why shouldn't it look well?" said Anne peevishly. "Don't be silly, Sarah. When you are silly, you are so very silly!"

Poor Sarah giggled, and thought how amusing

it was to tease Anne. The little creature would revel in these minute jests which she alone knew and which she only could understand. They were her secrets, and, when other women in society looked wise over their ambitious schemes and amorous intrigues, Sarah felt no less blessed and equally mysterious with her tiny *rises* and *scores*, which, she thought, would startle the world very much could they have been made known. Oh, they *were* such fun! What a burden her conscience carried in those some four invisible jokes!

Warre was touched, yet not altogether bewildered, at the change in Anne. His experience forbade him to hope that it was more than a mood, and he dreaded the reaction. Yet how charming she was in those days! One morning she said to him:

"I want to win back your respect, dear."

He tried to love her. The monotony of the simple, regular life they were leading gave Anne a still excitement, just as one note repeated several times in music, insisted on, accentuated, long drawn out, soothes the ear for the inevitable lower fall or shriller pitch in the tone. When will it come? What sound will it be? The girl's spirit grew outwardly calmer; her face regained its almost angelic beauty, borrowing innocence from the peaceful atmosphere which breathed around her. And as her affection for Simon became more honest, she had no wish to indulge in the studied coquetries which women play off against such men, who, vain themselves, only appeal to a woman's vanity. The native asceticism in Warre's character exercised the same fascination for her which the ascetic invariably exerts over the worldly and self-indulgent. It is one of the profound laws in the economy of human nature— this tribute of the flesh to the spirit. Warre's patience, kindness of disposition, generosity, and devotion to his work often filled Anne with envious exasperation; she watched him, lynx-like, for a moment of self-betrayal. But although he sometimes spoke hastily, and showed, on occasions, a quick temper, the more she observed the tenor of his daily life, the more she believed in his integrity. With tears in her eyes she would tell Sarah that poor old Simon was a born saint. It was no credit to him that he was so good, however, because there was nothing bad in his heart. *Darling, unnatural pet! Cold intellectuality!* She never supposed that the poor fellow ever had an instinct to curb, a passion to control, or a word to check; she knew nothing of the struggles in his soul, or of the atrocious mental suffering which racked his strong nature—as strong in its possibilities for evil as in its aspiration towards the right. She knew nothing of the all but irresistible temptations which pursued him—sometimes with relentless cruelty, sometimes with a sly persistence, sometimes withdrawing altogether for an easeful period, only to return again with renewed strength and greater cunning. But she began to understand his handsome face, and, when a former lover once passed her carriage in the Row, she thought him brutally coarse, and wondered why she had ever admired a type so unrefined. She determined, too, to gain her victory over Simon. When she read Shakespeare to him in the evening, she would find out, by artless questions, what qualities he admired in the heroine, and, when works of art were reproduced in the illustrated journals, she observed the types of beauty which pleased him most. He was touched, but not deceived, when she talked in the tender strain of Imogen, attempted the wit of Beatrice, and dressed her hair like Romney's Lady Hamilton. Who could deny the childish grace with which she told her unintentional, purely spontaneous lies; or who could think, when she blushed and glanced aside, that she was really responsible for all that she said and did under the stress of passion? Sometimes she sang sad songs till his heart nearly broke with their pathos, and she trilled ballads from Shakespeare and Shelley till the voice seemed the words, and the words the woman, and all their exquisite beauty, her own He also began to believe in her affection for himself, and he was one who craved and longed for sympathy as only men who are called self-reliant can crave it. But it was not in Anne's conscience to be faithful; she belonged to the eternal race of Molly Seagrims; such women are at the mercy of every comely libertine, and every comely libertine is at their mercy; they are lightly caught, and as lightly they escape. Warre knew that if he wished to possess any permanent influence over Anne it was only to be held by maintaining an almost inhuman reserve—a passionless indifference. Like all those with whom love has degenerated into a capricious instinct, she had a secret contempt for those who were appealed to by her fascination. She never felt a sincere trust in Warre until she learnt that he was not to be won by tricks and flatteries.

One day she met, in the hall, a lady who rustled past her, reeking of patchouli, and swaying her elaborate petticoats. She recognised her as Mrs. Bolingbroke. Anne ran into Warre's study with white cheeks.

"She is not a patient," she panted; "she pretends to consult you about old Wenslow, but she will try and make love to you. I know the creature! I have every confidence in you; I will never say a word about your ideas—perhaps it is as well you have them, for I am very jealous, and I would have no one come between us. You are mine! No other woman shall take you from me! You are mine!" . . .

Wickenham had gone abroad, and Warre now saw no one except his colleagues at the hospital and his patients. So busy a man was not expected to play an active part in society, and Anne delighted those who were old-fashioned by her apparent devotion to her husband and her home. Simon's relatives conceded that his hasty marriage was, in every sense of the word, a success, and, having more amusing topics and people to claim their attention than a well-matched couple who showed every desire to be let alone, they dismissed him from their minds.

"The Warres," they said, "are charming, but so self-centred."

Sir Hugh and Lady Delaware, however, dined with the young people every Sunday. The Baronet would carry away his supply of cigars for the week, and her ladyship would give advice which usually created a tornado in the kitchen for three mornings out of the seven. Simon would laugh, for, on the whole, things went smoothly.

But when only two weeks remained of the London season, Anne declared that her drawing-room was habitable, and surprised Warre by sending out three hundred invitations to an evening party. Many of them were his own acquaintances; some were Sarah Dane's; the rest were artistic celebrities whom Anne herself had known before her marriage, and to whom she now showed an ostentatious friendliness. The lesser lights among them eat her supper with an ill-humoured appetite, and those who were more distinguished, finding three Cabinet Ministers and a neat selection from the Peerage in the throng, remained longer than they had intended. But the entertainment was not a success. It injured Warre in his profession, where he was already somewhat unpopular, on account of his aristocratic connections and his youth; they said *he was coming on too fast*. The aristocratic connections, on the other hand, were not disposed to welcome a rival hostess in the person of any Mrs. Simon Warre. Her husband made a decent income, but he had neither the position nor the wealth to play any prominent part in the world of fashion. Several leaders of society allowed it to be understood that they would not in future find it convenient to grace the Grosvenor Street receptions. It was not right to encourage a foolish young couple in living beyond their means. The doctor's wife dressed far too richly for her station; *she might have been the Queen of Sheba;* and she showed bad taste in keeping all the best men round her own chair. *They could not get away from her.* Then let her have the men, by all means. When women are driven to grant this liberal concession they mean mischief.

Morning after morning, noon after noon, night after night, Anne watched the post for the notes of invitation which did not come. The wives of Simon's colleagues had found her too patronising; she had offended for ever three dowagers by her tiara, and her smile had been too intelligent at four other ladies whose husbands were called indulgent. Anne ground her pretty teeth, and, dressing more elaborately than ever, sat with Sarah Dane or Lady Delaware in the Row, to force salutations from a large acquaintance who, although they hated, could not cut her. Mrs. Dane as a rich, not old, virtuous, and amiable widow, had an euphonious visiting list as long as two arms, but, while she was highly esteemed, she was neither ambitious nor clever, her own sex found her dull, and men, the sort of woman you can only marry. Her chair in the park was treated with distant reverence, and when Anne sat by her side in all her defiant beauty, hats were lifted and gentle bonnets bowed with perhaps too marked a direction toward the widow. It was hard to bear. If only Lord Wickenham were in town! He came of too ancient a family to be a snob; he was Simon's dearest friend, and would not, Anne felt sure, see his friend's wife treated so unkindly. He would have invited them to his dinner parties, his house parties, and on his yacht; he ruled supreme in his own set, for he was so independent of them all; he was rich, he was a bachelor. Oh, why did he not return to be her champion?

The senior physician at the Hospital fell seriously ill, and Simon was obliged to remain in the town for the whole summer. Sarah Dane went to St. Moritz with the Duchess of Wark; even Sir Hugh and Lady Delaware took their annual three weeks' leave; Warre's mother, Lady Henrietta, and her husband, the Rev. Mountstuart Thompson, had long been absent from England at one of the large towns in the South of France, where he was British Chaplain, and where her ladyship, as his invalid but talkative wife, made him a much commiserated man.

August, September, and half of October passed. Anne no longer offered to read aloud in the evenings, and she no longer sang. Nothing amused her. She thought no more either of love or lovers; ambition, for the time, was her ruling passion, and, unable to gratify it, she pined. Warre was yet handsome in her sight, and, when she felt in the humour, she could still distract herself by trying to please him. But she was so rarely in the mood. She would lie for an hour at a time on the floor of her room, face downwards, with clenched hands, biting the dust, praying for triumph over her enemies. She had a superstitious belief in the power of prayer. Warre found her senseless in her boudoir one day with a bottle of chlorodyne in one hand and a paper bearing the words "*I am tired of life*" in the other. She soon revived; women like Anne only commit suicide by accident. They never mean to swallow more than an indiscreet dose of any poison; their object is not to kill themselves, but to alarm others. Warre was not terrified; his distress was something deeper than terror.

"Why do you make yourself so wretched?" he said.

"I hate the world!" she sobbed; "women are all such cats and the men are all such cowards. If

I had been born an heiress, London would have been at my feet. But because I am only your wife, and because I am beautiful, they want to trample me down. They are like wild beasts. And I am no *parvenue*," she added, drying her eyes. "The Delawares and Pavenhams were mostly blackguards, and they never brought much virtue to any house" (she had the decency to blush as she owned this), " but they were certainly distinguished ; they were men who fought for their country, and women of high caste, who, if they sometimes loved too well, had the courage to admit it."

Anne drew herself up with the traditional dignity of a traditional queen in exile.

"And I am no adventuress," she continued. "I demand my right place in society, and I will have that place. Becky Sharpes and Madame Bovarys fail because they try to get where they do not belong. But I am only asking for my due. I will not come down to the nobodies ; they have no mind, no taste, no spirit ; they are afraid of each other ; they are dull, pompous fools ! They were forced upon me when I lived in that detestable boarding-house, and they loathed me because they saw I did not bear their stamp. I was born to meet people who know how to use this world ! I will not be cheated of my birthright. But, oh !

how hard it is to be obliged to fight for what is lawfully your own!"

All the night she paced her floor, weaving impossible schemes of revenge and yet more impossible modes of battle. But she concealed these plans from Warre, who had a great contempt for such vulgar and ignominious nonsense. She made it a rule, too, never to *ask the advice of a failure*. She regarded him as a social failure. Why had he not gone into Parliament—as his mother had so wisely counselled? He had the makings of a fine speaker; his presence, too, was in his favour. What was a doctor? Bah! Simon had thrown away his life.

The following Sunday, Warre was called to the north of England for a consultation. He left her with great unwillingness, but he was to return early on Monday morning; he would take the night train; he would be absent twenty-four hours—not more.

"I must go," he said, "because it is my duty."

"And we really need the money," added Anne. "I have a few bills, darling."

She kissed him twenty times good-bye, shed a few tears, and said *God bless you!* She really felt sad over the parting, and it was a certain happiness to the poor man to find that she had need of him;

that he had become, as it were, a necessary, not altogether disagreeable, factor in her daily existence; he was her keeper, her tower of refuge. She would miss him. And how pleasant it is to be missed!

"Remember," he said, "that I shall be thinking the most charming things about you all the time I am away."

"Will that be hard work?" she asked, putting up her hands to be kissed.

He looked at her tenderly, and she smiled like a naughty child surprised by a little praise.

She gave him his gloves, and, standing on tiptoe, crowned him with his hat. All her gestures had a regal intention.

"Dearest," she said, "aren't we funny?"

As he drove away, she stood at the window, waving her handkerchief, and crying in earnest. He was the only creature in the world she honestly cared for; the only man she believed was not wholly selfish, brutal, and mercenary. It cost her an effort to control her emotion at the thought that there might be some accident on the railway. Oh, if he should be killed! She gave a little scream, and covered her eyes. Presently she seized his photograph from the mantelpiece, kissed it with frenzy, muttering the sweetest vows of affection and faith, and at last said:

"There is no one like you! I love you! I adore you! So handsome! So kind! So good! I worship you, darling! My husband! My prince! I wish you were richer! I wish you held a better position! Pet! Angel!"

Then, feeling tired, she rang the bell, and ordered word to be sent to the stable, that, when the brougham returned from the station, she wished to go for a drive. She went to Richmond.

The day was lost in fog. Through the leafless aisles of black, desolate trees in Hyde Park, she could only see stray couples pass and disappear like the figures in a shadow-dance. Those who were on the footpath near the carriage seemed to have gutta-percha faces—a few twisted into a crazy grin, and more convulsed with that hollow woe of a tragic mask. Sometimes a scarlet coat shone out like a stain of bright blood in the gloom. The water of the Serpentine could not be seen at all; its curves were lost under a wide and treacherous stretch of mist, profound, interminable. Dead brown foliage lay scattered on the grass near the road, but here and there, on a withered blade or leaf, the frost shone, opalescent. A soft line of purple vapour seemed to sever these unexpected, radiant corners from the oppressive atmosphere around.

A lady with rouged cheeks, pencilled eyebrows, and dyed hair, driving a pair of piebalds in a Stanhope, dashed down the Row. She looked exultant; she wore a hard hat like a man's, and the collar of her overcoat was drawn high over her ears. How she cracked her whip! How swiftly the wheels turned! How cold her little groom looked in his smart new livery! A great rattle, a clatter, and she passed out of sight. Two stout old men in a dog-cart halted at the Albert Memorial; one blew his nose; one yawned; they could see nothing, and their fat pony was restive. They rolled on.

In the Kensington High Street the fog was less dense. Bells were ringing for morning service at St. Mary Abbott's; many dim, respectable forms were entering the porch. Opposite, a woman who coughed, and who carried a child at her breast, was selling violets. When Anne passed Holland House she looked enviously at its gate. Ah! why was she not a Lady Holland? Why could she not have a salon? For a time she saw nothing on the road, but sat engrossed in her own bitter meditations, which were always the same, and which made her feel as though her heart were a nest of serpents. At last she looked up in time to see a young woman step into a hansom and smile as she told the cabman where to go.

"Ah," thought Anne, "she is going to enjoy herself! And here am I all alone! Why can't I have a little happiness?"

Oh, those dingy villas facing those cheap shops! Who lived in them? A girl with her sweetheart stood on the front steps of one. She looked contented enough, miserable creature! What wretched minds these common people had, or they would never endure such penury, such a narrow outlook! She began to cry, but brightened again when a woman on Hammersmith Bridge looked on her beauty and her equipage with dolorous envy. How well she knew this drive to Richmond! Dane and she had often dined at the Star and Garter; he dared not take her to more fashionable haunts; and there she used to parade the extravagant gowns he considered it injudicious to display in London. There, too, if they met an acquaintance, it would usually be in circumstances when no one of the party would be likely to mention the encounter. Ah! after all, she had enjoyed those days with Algernon. She had made him spend his money. She was not a woman like Sarah, to see how little expense she could be to a man. That was a fatal policy. Men never valued society which cost nothing. A group of young clerks were resting, with their bicycles, on the road. They all stared hard at Anne, mistaking her for some distinguished actress. She held her head high and struck a picturesque pose.

When the river appeared at Lonsdale Road, she wondered why people ever committed suicide by jumping into the water. How cold! how dirty! She drew her fur rug higher over her knees, and pulled her velvet mantle more close at the throat. A few yards ahead she saw a couple walking; the woman was leaning with pathetic confidence on the man's arm. Anne looked well at them; she always studied lovers. The girl was sweet; she ought to have been in the ballet at the Empire —not wasting her time and her beauty on that frightful little clerk, with weak eyes and no chin! What a hard world this was for pretty women! But who is that? A gaily attired youth, with a flower in his button-hole, drove past in a tandem. He was laughing to himself. He was in love with some one. What was she like? He, no doubt, was going to see her. Some of these vulgar creatures—when they happened to have money —got a great deal of amusement out of life. And he was not at all bad-looking. Ah! it was nice to be expecting some fine young fellow to call and take you for a drive.

"I am getting very sick of this kind of thing!" she said to herself.

Richmond Park at last! It seemed more drear than London. A few Cockney equestrians were cantering over the turf, but they were so plain and ungainly that Anne glanced away, regardless of their admiration. She told her coachman to drive towards the Robin Hood Gate. The air was chill and penetrating; a few deer were nibbling the green; the gaunt trees, uncouth and many-armed, looked in the fog like the black skeletons of deformed giants. Atmosphere and sky were one impenetrable cloud; the grass was patched by clumps of withered brown ferns.

She said to herself:—

"Is this life? Where is the fun?"

She met a number of young men with dogs. The women were probably at church. Church was all very well . . . sometimes. Presently she got out and walked. The way towards Kingston had more charm; the mist had a bluer tone; the trees were more slender, more symmetrical, and the green moss round their trunks, sparkling with dew, made her think of emeralds set in diamonds.

The undulation in the road was pleasant; she enjoyed the tramp up the hill, and began to grow sentimental on the subject of dead Algernon and the absent Warre. She tried to remember a certain line of Browning's about "*Never the time, the place, and the loved one being together*," and was deeply touched. Then she re-entered the carriage, and drove in a sullen apathy—looking neither toward the right nor to the left—toward the Star and Garter.

As she approached the building her colour rose; she scanned each window eagerly. There was no one in sight. One could see nothing of the famous view; two tall, bare poplar trees, like the sentinels of Destiny, were all that was conspicuous. She felt an unreasonable disappointment. Why had she been feeling *strange presentiments?*

She saw nothing on the way home, but thought vaguely of vague things. Once or twice she thought she must be asleep and dreaming.

Was this life? Where was the fun?

These two questions were the clearest that she asked herself that day. She asked them very often, and could find no acceptable answer.

CHAPTER XVI

A Prelude

ANNE had ordered for her luncheon several costly delicacies and a bottle of champagne, because her dear love was away and she felt so lonely. The food and the fruit seemed delicious; the wine gave her a languorous content. In the afternoon, she drove out again, dressed up in a gorgeous new pelisse, which was lined with the richest brocade and trimmed with ermine. Her little bonnet was made of ermine, too, and had a green parrot's wing, studded with red glass rubies, on either side. She was proud of her brilliant complexion, and wore no veil. She had added three false coils to her already abundant hair. Every one stared as her carriage rolled by.

In Bond Street she saw a man whom she knew. She had made his acquaintance at a City dinner where she had sung the year before. He had asked to be presented to her on that occasion, and had shown a disposition to encourage art. He was a rich Australian. Should she bow now? Their glances met. He at once motioned to her coachman to stop. Anne smiled at his audacity.

He was a man of that dashing type which, secretly, she most admired. He was tall; he had bold eyes; his clothes were like those of a fashionable comedian in the character of a captain in the Guards. Lifting his glistening hat, he displayed a fine picturesque head and Hyperion curls. He took her hand.

"Ah!" he murmured, with a meaning smile, "why did you not write that time—as you promised?"

"You see," she answered, "I married!"

He was amazed. His look had said, as he surveyed her carriage, "I was fully prepared to provide for you quite as handsomely."

"Didn't you see it in the papers?" she asked. "But perhaps you only know my professional name. My father is Sir Hugh Delaware. My husband is Dr. Warre."

"Well, I never!" ejaculated her friend. "I am sure I congratulate you. Sir Hugh Delaware! And Warre—that's the swell on paralysis. He has cured one or two of my directors! Sir Hugh Delaware! What a world it is! Fancy meeting you here after all these months! Talk about fate! When can I call and see you?"

She had not intended this. He was not an acquaintance she wished to encourage; he was not in a good set; he had a common accent. But then he was enormously rich; was married, and had four children. What could be more respectable?

"How is Mrs. Lumley Savage?" she asked, kindly.

He pulled a mournful face.

"Ah, my poor wife!" he said. "She has always been delicate since our first boy was born, and the last has destroyed her nerves altogether. We are extremely anxious about her health."

"I must call on her," said Anne, with regal graciousness.

"Do. She is always at home. She misses the Australian climate. . . . But where do you hang out? Will you be in this afternoon?"

"My husband is away," murmured Anne.

"So much the better," cried the gallant, with a grin. "I am not coming to talk science! Shall we say five o'clock?"

She nodded her head, and stifled a laugh in her muff. Savage coloured red from the force of his admiration for her blue eyes. They rebuked . . . challenged . . . surrendered . . . and defied in one deep twinkle.

"By Jove!" said he.

She put down her muff and looked as demure as his own little girl, aged four.

"At five," repeated Anne.

She bowed. He stepped back. The coachman drove on.

CHAPTER XVII

The Unlovely

WARRE returned on the morrow by a later train than the one he had named on leaving, and Anne walked, muttering, from room to room, awaiting his arrival. When he came, she ran to meet him in the hall, and, as he crossed the threshold, screamed reproaches. What did this mean? Why had he not kept his word? Who believed telegrams? Did he think she was a fool? She followed him into his study.

She was not dressed so carefully as usual, but looked a slattern in an old red velvet gown she sometimes wore when she was not at home to callers, or when she practised. Her face, distorted by anger, resembled nothing human; she had tangled her hair into a mad disorder; and her eyes, struggling in their sockets, darted wildly from side to side like strange living things of some existence separate from her own. She was horrible to look at.

Warre picked up his letters; she snatched them from his hand.

"Put them down!" she said. "Listen to me! I will be treated with respect!"

She shouted; she swore; her words were fragrant with brandy. Warre wondered whether Algernon Dane could have taught her the language she used. He had talked the slang of third-rate debauchees—a jargon which is often nasty, but never robust.

"How did you spend the time yesterday?" asked Simon.

She had been for a drive. In the evening, she had attended service at Westminster Abbey. After church she had gone to supper at the Savoy—with some old friends.

"Who were they?"

He had never heard her speak of them. They were rich colonials—Mr. and Mrs. Lumley Savage. The wife was consumptive, poor thing, and had four lovely children. The husband—oh, he was a bore! But why all these questions? She was not in the witness box! Perhaps he had better have her watched by a detective. No doubt he had already taken that precaution. Saintly men and invalid wives were usually sneaks and spies. With an atrocious laugh, she drummed a tattoo on the table. What did she care? What did it matter? She continued her abuse.

The servants, with white looks, stood on the kitchen staircase to listen. In the end, Anne feigned a swoon and sank on the floor. Warre waited for her restoration to consciousness, and endured her relapse into maudlin remorse and hysterical affection. A suspicion so horrible possessed him that he dared not trust himself to ask her more about the yesterday.

She sang ballads all that evening, and called him unsympathetic, because he did not seem to enjoy her rendering of a song set to some lines by Swinburne :

> "Let come what will, there is one thing worth,
> To have had fair love in the life upon earth;
> To have held love safe till the day grew night,
> While skies had colour and lips were red."

From that time forth Anne apparently made no attempt at self-control.

She grew slovenly, yet more extravagant; bolder in her lies, and more regular in her attendance at church; more plausible in the world and more shameless at home; every day she indulged in some wild burst of temper; she was too passionate to be a mere shrew—her wrath was like a stage storm—violent and abrupt, heralded by moonlight and immediately followed by the noonday sun. The servants dreaded her step; Warre suffocated in her presence; the house was a hell. Sarah now called rarely, as she was much engrossed with the affairs of a hospital which she was having built at Ventnor in memory of Algernon Dane. Anne, no longer ambitious, collected together a group of friends who only lived to be seen at the Savoy and have it rumoured that some one paid their bills. How gorgeously they dressed! How loudly they laughed! And the women wore Court *coiffures* in the style which is inseparably associated with the Royal House in England. It was a world of Christian names and pagan nakedness. Mrs. Lumley Savage played the part of blind poodle, and followed Anne with servile assiduity. She was a silly, vain, vulgar, but harmless little creature, who felt aristocratic sensations thrill through her moral being whenever she remembered that Mrs. Warre was the daughter of a baronet. She experienced an agreeable awe in Anne's society; copied her insolent manners, her gaudy clothes, her large hand-writing, her bouncing gait, and, when they were in places of amusement together, they talked, in languid but far-reaching tones, of *Tom, not the Duke of Drawne but the Duke of Daleham*, and *poor*

Mary, who would marry Lord de Trappe. They often went shopping together, and then they found it a great pleasure to be stared at by admiring footmen on the steps of Marshall & Snelgrove's. Warre could rarely spare his brougham in the afternoon, so Anne always used "Nellie's" carriage, which was yellow, and lined with satin, and swung on Cee-springs. There were numerous brass ornaments, like coronets, on the harness, and the horses—which stepped so high that it took them an hour to get round the Park—wore bearing-reins and ribbon rosettes. They looked like circus steeds, and were rich in foam and froth; they had been trained to rear, to plunge, to toss their heads and paw the ground. When Anne was in a great hurry, she almost preferred a hansom. Lumley Savage himself never came to Grosvenor Street; Anne explained that he was not a person who cared for society. He was a man's man—*a company promoter or something*—and entertained great City princes at a house in Portman Square, which he had hired, furnished, for that purpose. His wife was always considered too great an invalid to appear on these occasions; she preferred to be seen at Mrs. Warre's, reclining on a sofa, and smiling at an endless train of politicians not in Parliament; musicians who could not play, writers who never wrote, and handsome bachelors who never married. Yet Anne's conduct was, in many respects, irreproachable She never flirted. It was owned that of all young married women she was the most discreet with her admirers. She was considered vain, but virtuous.

Ten months passed. As sailors drink sea-water to cure their nausea, Warre read the ugliest literature, took his exercise in the dirtiest slums, and brooded on the most repulsive aspects of disease. Refinements of language jarred on his disappointed ears; the obscene song which a boy had sung under his window, on the day of his fatal marriage, seemed the one great psalm in existence. Oh, had the time gone for ever when he could step out and say, in homely, uninspired commonplace :

"The day is clear, the sky is blue, the flowers smell sweet"?

When it was dark, he would sometimes steal into the Catholic Church in Farm Street, and rest there, undisturbed. He used to sit near the altar of Our Lady of Lourdes, where he could see, at the end of the aisle, another altar and the pendent lamps before it. The odour of flowers, incense, melting wax, and that something else like the scent of goodly fruit stored away for the hungry winter, gave him a welcome. He felt that he was in some way expected, that his place was set ready; that there were loving friends on every side who had been waiting, watching, longing for his approach. And while he could stay there, in his small, unmolested corner, it seemed that neither sorrow nor pain, hopes overthrown nor miseries multiplied, could ever harm him more. The little silver hearts which hung in a case by the altar had each some story to tell of a faithful vow. And should he be faithless! He forgot his own narrow grief as he mused on the great sufferings of men, who, if human joys were given to truth and honour, deserved every perfect gift. It seemed to him that his own aims had been common and selfish; he felt an ineffable humiliation before the symbols of martyrdom which gave the walls of that sacred place a vivid pathos. His ways were pure because his nature was chivalrous, but his life was worldly. His youthful ambition had been to make money and fame, to marry a beautiful wife; he had loved passing well the pleasures of earth, fair women, wealth, and the luxuries wealth alone can promise. How much had he done or endured just for righteousness' sake?

The peace Warre found in these exalted moments at church only made his own hearth seem a more sordid reality—a crueller disillusion. We do not think of our deserts, but of our unfulfilled desires, when existence looks desolate.

He decided that it was not suicide to perish from overwork. He undertook the duties of two men, and performed them with the energy of three. His colleagues often named his probable successor. He was not yet thirty, and he looked old. He began to stoop ; his tread was swift—not with eagerness—but with the desperation of a hunted creature. What was the matter with Warre ? Did he ever laugh now, ever sleep, ever rest ? How long could he last ? Women said that he was wretched at home ; some of them tried to make his existence happier by blushing into it. More than one pretty romantic soul gave him glances which would have melted an anchorite. But had he cared for the consolations of patchouli, was not Anne herself the fairest of false lights o' love ? And he still possessed some influence over her heart ; corrupt as she was, she would have been baser without him. She had woven fear, love, and hatred into one dense passion, which, had he loved her in return, would soon have become hate only.

CHAPTER XVIII

Wickenham

ONE day in December, Simon received a letter from Wickenham. It was dated from the English Embassy at Rome, where he was a guest. Anne looked over Warre's shoulder as he read it and clapped her hands.

"So he is coming to town at last," she said. "Now we shall see a change! But what a year I have spent! I am sure I deserve a little amusement! If you observe the workings of Providence, you will generally find them fair."

Her ambition revived; she began to hate Mrs. Lumley Savage.

The day his lordship called Anne received him in the drawing-room, where she sat with a crystal vase of orchids on the table by her side, and, behind her head, a cushion embroidered with peacock's feathers. Her gown was of silk the colour of honey, and worked with beads which looked like precious stones; the belt glittered with arrows and serpents, stars and crescents, turquoise, opal, and amethyst pins and clasps. Rings shone on her fingers, and a comb of paste diamonds in her hair. Warre had not yet returned from the hospital. She told Wickenham about her social disappointments with a naïve and childish petulance which amused him. He thought her silly yet beautiful, and felt that she was, on the whole, a victim to feminine malice.

"Saxon women," he said, "are very good to their men, but they are brutal to each other."

She fell into that familiar tone which members of the same caste, calling, or family instinctively adopt when they are alone together.

"Make them nice to me," she said, with tears in her voice. "I do so want to be liked! My disposition is friendly. I love the life of show and hospitality; I was born for it. The wife of a professional man cannot be foolishly exclusive; I have to entertain many people whom I could scarcely ask even my own relatives to meet! I think it most unjust, however, for my set to abandon me merely because I have to be civil—in my husband's interest—to outsiders. Simon says nothing, but, I assure you, he feels it deeply. His pride is hurt; the unkindness I have received has made him ill.

You will see the change in him at once. I am so anxious ... about his health."

Her lips quivered; one little foot, in its lace stocking and golden slipper, nervously tapped the ground.

"Could I speak like this?" she said, "could I mention these slights ... if I were not driven to it by worry? After all, what do I care for society? Of course, it is pleasant to meet refined and cultured minds—to associate with one's equals. I am young, too. Is it a crime to enjoy a dance or a dinner with men and women who take my point of view for granted; who think, feel, and believe as I do? I get so tired of explaining life to middle-class intellects! I always feel as though I talked Greek, and they only knew Dutch, and we were trying to sing a French duet! Yet I could bear isolation, *ennui*, anything, if only Simon would look happy. But he does not. It is his nature to feel more for others than they feel for themselves. For every scratch I have been given he has two scars! He seems to think that I resigned a—a brilliant future to marry him. But what did it matter to me what his position was, or his family, or his mother's unfortunate *mésalliance*? My parents, certainly, disapproved of my marriage. Mamma is old-fashioned—she is a true

Pavenham. She cannot forget the uncle who has a draper's shop. Have you ever seen him? Is he hopeless? I am so glad that he lives at Scarborough!"

"I have met him," said Wickenham, gruffly. "He is a quiet, unpretentious sort of fellow . . . certainly presentable. But in any case I should stick up for him because he has behaved so awfully well to Warre!"

Anne leant forward, with a flattering and eager admiration in her regard.

"Ah!" she cried, "if all men and women were as generous as you and my dear Simon! But they are not; they make the most ill-natured remarks."

"What can it matter what a cad thinks?" said his lordship. "I never trouble about 'em. Let 'em say what they like about Warre or Warre's uncle. The only people who listen to 'em are other cads. No friend of mine has ever even mentioned the—the Scarborough relative. And, as a matter of fact, he can't be called a regular shopkeeper. The shop is so large! It's almost wholesale. I should be very glad if one of my Irish cousins could—could get hold of something half as good. I shouldn't mind a bit. Lord Blarney, my mother's nephew, sells mutton—thin, stringy stuff—and he can't make it pay. My housekeeper makes an awful row when I ask her to get her meat from Blarney. But you must be loyal to your own!" He gave her an odd glance as he spoke.

"I wish," she said prettily, "I had always known some one who could . . . scold me . . . like this . . . and make me feel a mean, sickly little snob."

With a bewitching gesture, she covered her rosy cheeks with her two white hands. Wickenham wished to dislike her, but could not. He had heard about her vulgarity, her extravagant frocks, *her loud style, her fast companions,* from the Duchess of Wark and other lady friends. He saw why few women would care for her. He felt that no man could find it possible to judge her severely. She had irresistible charms. True, her gown was startling, but the whole effect was picturesque and Oriental. Possibly one would not like one's wife to look so—brilliant, but that was a personal fad. It went for nothing.

"I have not scolded you!" he replied.

"You spoke from your heart."

"I really forget what I said. Wasn't it something about Blarney's mutton?"

"You have helped me so much—made so much that was difficult, easy!"

"Good Lord!" he ejaculated.

He looked about him, and then said gravely:

"How does Wiggin answer as a footman?"

Wiggin was the son of one of his pensioners at Weyborough. He asked fatherly questions about this youth till Warre came in.

Anne left the two friends together.

They seemed to have little to add after the first common questions had been warmly asked and replied to, but, with furtive, curious glances, each scanned the other's face. Both men had changed since their last meeting. Warre was still handsome; his eyes still shone with their peculiar piercing brilliancy. He had aged, however, and was sallow; his mouth wore the hard bit of a continual self-restraint. Wickenham looked well; the breezy air of patrician indifference which had kept his humanity too cool had now more of the sun and less of the world and its dust; his innate kindness had mellowed into courteousness; his innate seriousness, into a glad serenity.

"I wonder you left the South," said Warre, at last; "it is such a bad time to come back. How long were you in Rome?"

"Three weeks. Shanklin makes an excellent Ambassador, and Lady Shanklin is delightful. But then her great-grandmother was not English;

that is why she understands that a *grande dame* should be distinguished for small talk! I am not very keen about our Northern women. They are so bleak. They can bow down to a superior and be gracious with the poor, but there is not one in a hundred who knows how to behave toward her equals. It is a touch of the gipsy—a drop of alien blood, or a hint of the Celt—that tells!"

Warre sighed. Wickenham continued:

"Your friend, Count Vendramini, dined with us several times. He spoke rather coldly of you, and said you had not written once since your marriage. How's that? I suppose you have had so much to do. He saw your signature attached to all the Duke of Hothenstein's bulletins, so he knew you were alive! Vendramini's daughter," he added, in another tone, "is considered one of the Roman beauties. She refused Prince Alberoni last month. I admire her spirit. It would have been a brilliant marriage—considered socially—for any woman. But she is unlike others. . . . I should not have left Rome if she had not been leaving it too, this week."

He paused. His lordship was not a man to betray his thoughts when he wished to conceal them. He spoke now with a marked deliberation.

"She is coming to spend the winter in London

with her god-mother, Lady Ralston of Braddyck. She lives at Morne House, near Kew."

He stood up, walked away, and came back again.

"I am not sentimental, as you know," said he, "but I feel as though all my happiness depended on ... on some one else. I am awfully hard hit!"

It was growing dark; Wickenham could not see the pallor of Warre's face. And he was pale himself from striving to speak without passion this new so passionate interest in his life.

"I am awfully hard hit!" he said again; "I wonder why you never mentioned her. She is so beautiful."

"As I remember her," said Warre, like one in a dream, "she had dark hair and eyes."

"Black hair and large brown eyes."

"Her features were delicate."

"Sweet!"

"Is her face a shade too pale?"

"It is like a magnolia."

"I thought her a little too slight."

"Would you have a girl of nineteen look like one of Ruben's wives?"

"She was very shy!"

"I love her modesty! Oh, Warre, she is the

only woman I can marry! If she says No to me—and why should she say Yes?—I shall never think of any one else. I should not even feel tempted to think of any one else. That is always the way when you meet the one true queen. Even if she passes you by, you can never again be happy with mere usurpers. I'm a loyal subject, Simon. I serve but one mistress, and she must be the king's daughter! Do you remember our old talks?"

"Ho! ho!" laughed Warre. "Ha! ha! We were philosophers in those days. I was the Stoic, and you, 'the wiser Epicurean.' We read Plato, and Homer, and Newman, and Rabelais, and Montaigne, and a fine nourishing soup we made of them all! What have we *not* read, you and I? And what has it done for us, Wick? I am patching dead lives and you want to marry a wife! Ho! ho! ha! ha! the man in the street has a better time than either of us."

The servant entered with the tea-things, and spread out upon a table fantastic porcelain cups of richest gilt. The tray was of beaten copper; the little kettle, of silver picked out with brass; the small teapot, the jug for the cream, and the bowl which held the sugar were each of gold, enamelled with strange designs in crimson and green.

When these were arranged, the man drew the violet silk curtains across the window, and set a low chair of quaintly carved ivory and bright purple cushions for Anne. How unreal, unsubstantial, brittle it all seemed! Was it a scene that could last? Must it not perish soon, and fade away utterly like a vision in the night? Would the silk bear the dust of one year? Would those toys—those trifles in silver and gold—endure even water too hot, or a hand less light, less delicate than Anne's?

The wind howled through the house with a thrilling grief; and, in response, the woodwork seemed to murmur its remembrance of forest-sounds. The room, Warre thought, was surely filled with creeping things which hissed, flying things which stung, faces which leered and mocked, bats' wings, and the hoot of owls!

The door opened. Anne came in.

"How dark it is!" she exclaimed, and, as she spoke, turned light into the many opal lamps which hung on the wall.

She made the tea; she talked. Lord Wickenham thought her good company. They did not miss Warre's voice; he sat back in his corner, thinking, and was silent.

He had always told himself that Allegra must

marry; but now that the possibility looked so certain, all that was human in his affection for her arose. Jealousy gnawed at his heart with cruel fangs, and life seemed to beat upon his soul, like those harsh waves, which, on a rocky coast, bear a burden of blinding sand and small sharp stones. He was cold—ice-cold from head to foot, and when he held out his hands to the blazing coal, he only caught what seemed the north wind breathing down the chimney. The fire was as chill as the glitter of Anne's jewels.

To meet Allegra face to face again; he not free, and she perhaps loving another. What anguish on earth could be so cruel as that? The day had long passed when he could smile in bitter self-contempt at this one romantic passion in his history. Absence, distance, and the hopelessness of it all had only lifted it higher than common things, till, like a spirit set free from the cage of the world, it flew on unwearied pinions through endless sky, and, because unwearied, seeking no rest—no final halting-place. On, on for ever; more than content with its gift of perpetual energy—its perpetual release from the sorrow which makes happiness look too tempting, and from the happiness, which, once tasted, gives every sorrow the flavour of a death potion.

But Warre was a man, and young; he had too strong and too intense a nature to meet Allegra day by day and maintain self-mastery. Would the hopelessness always seem so hopeless? Would the barrier between them look so dense when hand touched hand? Would her eyes, as he drew near, be less like clouds of night and more like those of a woman he dearly loved? He feared the ordeal before him. There must be no love in his life —no wife. But work, and only work, until the end. How hard to remember that at nine-and-twenty!

Anne went to the piano. She played well when music was the only possible outlet for her emotions. She began to strike out chords which Warre had never heard before. Then they broke, like waves within waves, into melodies and counter-melodies. And as he listened, he thought of meadows where lovely flowers grew and of sunshiny orchards; gardens where young girls were laughing, chatting, dancing, pelting each other with primrose balls in the moonlight; knights in armour rushed past him on white horses, and he met Death, who was grave, with folded wings; and he met Youth, who was cross-gartered, tall, and comely, who sucked an orange while he read his lesson-book; and he met Love, whose feet were white and spotless, though the road was black with mire, and whose face was like the dawn, although the evening was come. The wind—how it moaned! And the rain never ceased! Mist, darkness, and yet a choir chanting in the distance ; the odour of incense and the sweet breath of pure air and spring ; the little laugh of water when it strikes a pebbly shore ; the trill of a brook running through fields to the sea ; the sound of many wings in the air, and then— Anne singing :—

> "Fear no more the heat o' the sun,
>   Nor the furious winter's rages ;
> Thou thy worldly task hast done,
>   Home art gone, and ta'en thy wages ;
> Golden lads and girls all must,
> As chimney-sweepers, come to dust.
>
> "Fear no more the frown o' the great,
>   Thou art past the tyrant's stroke ; —
> Care not more to clothe and eat ;
>   To thee the reed is as the oak :
> The sceptre, learning, physic, must
> All follow this, and come to dust.
>
> "Fear no more the lightning-flash,
>   Nor the all-dreaded thunder-stone :
> Fear not slander, censure rash ;
>   Thou hast finish'd joy and moan :
> All lovers young, all lovers must
> Consign to thee, and come to dust."

CHAPTER XIX

The Unspoken

THREE days later, Allegra arrived in London. Anne was disappointed in the fit of a new cloak, and, affecting a nervous headache, made that an excuse for not accomanying Warre when he called at Lady Ralston's. He was sorry. The dreaded meeting would have been less dangerous—if more humiliating—in Anne's presence. Had it been possible he would have avoided the renewal—which politeness now made obligatory—of his friendship with Count Vendramini's daughter. She rested in his memory like one whom he had passionately loved, but who no longer lived, and for whose loss he had spent the uttermost that was human and could suffer in his nature. If, after many years, the dead we have broken our hearts for could return to us—what should we say to them? What should we offer? Words which are only sounds, the arid stain of tears once shed, a teeming love drilled into a barren misery, arms which have clasped thin air too long to know how to embrace a friend. "Go back," one would say, "go back! I have forgotten how to be glad. I cannot welcome ye; I have nothing to say to ye." And perhaps they would leave us, and, as they disappeared again from our blind sight, we should feel again in our inanimate lives the old ache and agony, the torturing pulse of human grief. This, then, was the state of mind in which Warre found himself now that etiquette—that card-board goddess of peace—tripped in, as she always must, when we would have our tragedy austerely tragic. Simon had trained himself to think of Allegra—when he thought of her at all—not as a creature of flesh and blood—but as an influence to which he was wedded. Some men took the Church; some—Poverty for their bride; he had chosen ideal Love in the person of a living woman—just as Dante long ago had chosen Beatrice. Such a form of mental devotion is far more common than the married mortal passion that seems more general; but one belongs to the world invisible, the language of silence, the hidden being of a man; the other is evident, talkative, and, like the saint who prays in the market-place, it has its reward in the fact that it is a public profession—a privilege and a bliss known and observed by all who pass by.

As Simon drove towards Kew, he tried to read the *Lancet* and the *Times*; but although his eyes followed the print, its sense merely droned in his mind like the murmur of flies by a whirling river. Now his heart seemed to faint from the pinch of death; now it woke and throbbed with the pain of life. When he asked himself, Why? hot tears burnt up his laughter. When he said, "You are a sentimental fool!" the sharp knife of despair cut his breath. One sudden pang—more cruel than the rest—made him cry out. A moment later he was wondering—"Did that really hurt so much?" Sorrow broke him on her wheel. "This," he said, "is overwork! I must go into the country!"

And so he suffered and so he endeavoured to use his reason.

When love and wisdom fight there is always an open grave between them, and the vanquished is buried, under light leaves, alive. Both are immortal; both are invulnerable; there never is—there never can be—a victory, but one will sometimes grow tired and feign a surrender.

Some street musicians were playing the bridegroom's song from a new light opera. It was a joyous tune, giddy in strain but slow of measure. Warre knew the words; students and patients hummed them at the hospital. Night rhymed with bright; one parted never and loved for ever; the refrain was all about flowers and bowers, and *I am coming, my sweet, to thee!* The toiling, solitary youthfulness in Warre rose up in wild rebellion; that vulgar song told of the common joys which are given to make work possible. He had not slept well for many nights; he was rarely in bed before twelve, and he rose at seven; he was worrying about the domestic troubles of one of his colleagues; he suspected Anne of deceit and many things worse; debts were accumulating; he had endorsed a friend's bill for a large amount, and the friend had made bad investments. These money affairs alone were a constant fret. Oh, the weariness of it all! If he could only sleep—for a little while.

"Courage," he said to himself, "courage!" He set his face into the iron restraint which people not knowing his secret troubles mistook for pride—for hardness. What a pity it was, they would say, that Dr. Warre was so hard.

The portico of Morne House was supported by four Doric pillars, and, on either side, an inappropriate addition of bricks and mortar, cut into three long windows, jutted far enough from the original structure to form a balcony. The carriage-drive was moss-grown; the small but thickly planted shrubs which concealed each wing of the low mansion gave it a pinched—a shrunken aspect. The old servant who drew back the bolted doors was thin, cold, wheezing, and shabby. His nose, the tip of his chin, and the strained skin of his forehead were red, and he moved his shoulders as though his coat were chilling rather than a protection. Warre followed him through the hall, whose walls had that old-fashioned papering, which, varnished, is believed to resemble yellow marble. Here and there a magenta dampness shone out like a rich vein of rare mineral, and two plaster bas-reliefs, one, of Bacchus with nymphs, and the other, of Ariadne forsaken, were the sole decorations. But the bronze figure of an unbeautiful goddess stood at the foot of the staircase, supporting three unlit gas-jets on her crown, beckoning nowhere with one stern hand, and holding metal flowers in the other.

Simon found himself alone in the saloon. He saw many hard green velvet chairs, and smelt wild violets. A bunch of them stood in a little silver bowl on the "Davenport." Allegra must have gathered them, he thought. Their fragrance told the sweetness of her touch. At first he stood near the fire, and stared at the mantelpiece, which was held up by two marble divinities, whose limbs grew into a column, whose hands were apples, and whose breasts were true lovers' knots. They looked straight out into futurity with iris-less eyes, monuments of unpitying and unpitiful patience. The polished floor had grown dim, and the small rugs which warmed it looked frayed and faded. Dull satin striped with silk of a dingier tone hung on the walls. The ceiling was embossed with semi-circles, scrolls, and fleurs-de-lys in gilt. A large glass chandelier with glittering lustres hung in the middle, and was reflected in two of the four long narrow mirrows which divided each window. Outside there was a stone verandah, where leafless vines were shivering in the wind. Then came a gravel path, and then a stretch of lawn studded with empty urns, a few green bushes, and spreading fir trees. Beyond these was a paddock, where a few sheep were grazing; and beyond that, a row of tall bare elms, where the rooks had built their nests, and were cawing, cawing, flying hither and yon—black omens of good luck. The clouds in the distance seemed one with earth—a far-off country of high white hills—unpeopled and desolate. As Warre watched, he heard a light footstep in the hall. He turned his back to the light, and when Allegra entered, she could not see his face. But the glance of her eyes swept through him as though she were a skilled musician, and his heart a lute. She lived! she moved! She was no longer the bride of his sentiment, but bone of his bone, and flesh of his flesh, and soul of his soul. He trembled under the stress of that silent, unheard speech, that passionate, wordless language, which only finds utterance in the cry of the winds, and the tumult of the sea, and the falling of rain and sleet, or in the singing, buzzing, piping melodies of amorous Nature. Men and women alone have no eloquence when they love. Oh, why was it not possible to take her in his arms and say:

"*What has the world to give me while I have you? When you are absent, my beloved, I am blind, my day is darkness and my life is death; my hopes are all farewells, and my ambition is a mad bird with neither wings nor notes.*"

But instead he took her hand, which was so frail, so gentle, that he seemed to be holding a ray of the sun—nothing more—and said :

" I hope you are not feeling tired after your long journey? How is the Count?

" He is quite well," she answered.

Then, half in tears, she added, against her will :

"My dear Simon! My dear, dear Simon, how glad it makes me to see you again! Come and sit by the fire. My godmother is asleep just now. When she wakes they will call us. We have so many things to tell each other. Your marriage! It is so hard to think of you—in love!"

"Why?" he said flippantly. "I have been in love a dozen times!"

The tenderest of women can be cruel to a backward lover.

"A dozen times means never at all," said Allegra. "I see you know nothing about it!"

"You have never understood me."

"Nor have you ever understood me."

"Yet we are friends."

"Of course."

She was no longer the almost foolishly shy little girl of his days in Rome.

Warre was astonished at her self-possession, and chose to feel bitter—attributing the change to the fact that she had refused Prince Alberoni. Women were all alike, he thought. Even their virtues came to them through vanity. If Allegra seemed less proud, less distant, it was merely because she felt more sure of her power. Had he forgotten her beauty, or had she a new fascination? Her eyes were a softer depth; her mouth had lost its rather too prim precision, and her delicate figure had a charm it lacked before. The schoolroom dress was now a Parisian gown, blue lisse over dark green cloth ; its effect made him think of a flower he had never seen. Her fine, black hair was coquettishly dressed ; she had her own girlish grace, and with it that captivating worldliness of air which is so delicious a defect on an innocent countenance, and which is the most dangerous charm of a modish sinner. . . .

"Of course, we are friends," repeated Allegra ; "but I have sometimes thought that I may have seemed rather unkind when you were with us in Rome. And when you sent me the rosary, I wrote you a thankless letter."

Her face burned, but she continued:

" It was because we were so poor . . . and papa so often asked you why you did not marry ! He says the same thing to Lord Wickenham. And I am proud. . . . When a man has money or a good position, he rarely believes that any woman's . . . friendship . . . is disinterested. I almost wish that every man I knew was married ! I dare not be pleasant to a bachelor ! "

She laughed as she spoke, but her fingers clasped each other painfully.

" Papa has arranged to let the Palace to the

Cavernakes till the spring, and he has gone into partnership with an American who has a patent blacking—Belton's Bezonian Blacking! It is written all over Rome, and on Sunday afternoons they have bicycle races at the Borghese Villa between Belton's Bezonian and Barton's Elixir! Papa was never so happy in his life. He says he is making a fortune, and he hopes to be appointed Ambassador. He always wanted to represent Italy at the English Court. Poor papa! His American partner is a gentleman; he used to be the First Secretary of the United States Embassy in London! When he and papa are not writing advertisements, they talk about Art and religion, and play Poker! At first, I did not care for the blacking, but boots must be blacked, and there are a lot of boots! It seems a very honest way of earning money . . . and it is nice not to be a pauper. At one time I thought it would mean perfect contentment. But it doesn't. I have prettier clothes to wear, and my friends are more glad to see me . . . that is all."

Ah, why could she not speak out and tell of those days of grief, and loneliness, and cutting tears which had followed his departure from Rome? Why could she not say:

"*You are the only one I love; I can never love*

any other. Oh, I believe you love me, in spite of your coldness and your silence! I believed it even when you left me, and we looked at each other without words. But I have thought of you . . . always . . . always. I have stood at my window when all Rome was asleep, and held out my arms and said, 'Shall I never see you again? Why do you not come to me? Why will you not understand? Must I always be nothing to you . . . nothing? Oh, this foolish pride! Is it stronger than love? And this money piled up between us? Is it a mountain of brass? Why are you not poor, or why am I not rich?' I am no longer a little girl, my dearest. I have thought and suffered and wept since we last met. I have learnt to be alone—alone with my own troubles, my own doubts, misgivings, and cares; alone with my own laughter, my own sorrow, my own follies. But I will live true to my love, and so die in it that even Death will say, 'This woman has been faithful to her heart's one king!'"

But it was not possible to say this, and Allegra sat thinking sad things and laughing merrily.

"I suppose," said Warre, "you intend to pass a frivolous winter?"

No, she wished to be quiet. Her godmother was an old lady, who had spent half a century remembering four months of idyllic happiness. She was at once the torment and the angel of three parishes; to know her goodness one had to be suffering from poverty or an incurable disease. She had not a civil word for the prosperous. Allegra intended to devote herself to Lady Ralston's charities and missions. She had already ordered a pair of thick boots!

As Allegra talked, she drew her chair nearer the fire. Her slim, small foot, shod in silk and bronze kid, rested on the fender. There were little ruffles that looked like autumn leaves on the inch of underpetticoat which showed when she moved. Simon remembered Wickenham's once remarking that when virtue ceased to be dowdy, vice would lose all its allurement. He could imagine no Circe half so dangerous as this innocent witch of nineteen, whose deadliest art was an instinct for dainty attire.

Their conversation fell into that homely strain which is so sweet to men and women who live the greater part of their day in public, meeting friends who are the friends of some one else, murmuring artificial opinions on artificial subjects.

"I think you have been working too hard," said Allegra suddenly.

"Oh no. If I were not constantly occupied, I could not live at all."

Allegra grew pale, put out her hand as though she would touch him, and then drew it back.

"Don't say that!" she said. "Think of the women who have no work to keep them constantly occupied, and still—must live!"

It seemed to him that he could never again look away from her face. How beautiful the modelling of her cheeks, the transparent, fragile skin, the chiselled nose, the modest, silent mouth. She was neither witty nor brilliant. She had very little to say, because she spoke truth only. She was too gentle, too timid to make memorable remarks. Sometimes she showed a fairy's sense of humour, and sometimes a woman's untaught wisdom; but she did not know when she was amusing, and she would have been frightened had she guessed she could be profound. Allegra's charm was the charm of Spring-time and love; all the kind promises, the sunshine, the light, the tenderness, the warmth, the graciousness of Nature—none of her inexorable justice, her logical cruelty.

"I do not think you could argue well if you tried!" said Warre. "I don't believe you know anything about anything!"

And he laughed as he had not laughed for months. How he loved her!

"I believe," he went on, "that you could be sweetly unreasonable—that you could be perfectly absurd!"

He enjoyed making these commonplace, brotherly observations. Did they not signify a kind of intimacy? Did they not give him an excuse to watch her expressive countenance? She was not at all pleased; she said he was not to tease her; she became adorably cross. Her dark eyes flashed; colour swept into her face. Not reasonable! Absurd? Not know anything about anything? She was reading Dante and Shakespeare and Lord Rosebery's *Life of Pitt*.

"Pitt," said Warre. "Why Pitt?"

She blushed. Lord Wickenham had given her this extremely interesting work. He was teaching her English politics. Warre became more reserved, and, with a deep sigh, remarked that Wick was a fine fellow. Allegra replied that Lord Shanklin had called him *a very coming man*. Some one else at the English Embassy had said that he was Marcus Aurelius—without the naughty wife. What did that mean?

"Everybody wants him to marry," said Simon.

He glanced at her as he spoke. She was looking into the fire.

"I don't want him to marry," she said at length;

"he is one of my friends. It makes me jealous when my friends marry. I suffer."

"Have you not forgiven me . . . then?" he asked, pretending to jest.

She, too, pretended to jest, and said lightly:

"No. I still suffer; I am still jealous; I still remember the day your letter came . . . telling . . ."

His tone grew more careless, but his voice trembled.

"It must have been a very stupid letter"

Their eyes met.

"Tell me," she said, looking down, "tell me why you did it? Did you love her . . . so much? Was she so very pretty?"

"Yes . . . she is very pretty."

"Ah! . . . Well, I am not pretty. I may not be plain, but . . . do you think I am plain? I fancy I am better looking than I was . . . when you last saw me. That makes me feel rather happy! I did not get so jealous as I could, because . . . I was afraid it would make me ugly! I did not wish you to feel *quite* sure when we met that you had been wise to forget me. I wanted to look my best to-day. Do I?"

However unwise it may be to play the coquette after twenty, a maiden in her teens may follow this indiscreet instinct in the certain assurance of a full absolution. Women have but one manner when they wish to be admired, and they all have a longing for admiration—in some cases, of one man only, in other cases, of all men. Allegra was an innocent Anne; Anne was a vicious Allegra. Warre, who had been growing clear-sighted in these subtle distinctions since his marriage, now knew why he had first been drawn towards Anne, and why he must always love the young girl who now seemed so far away from his every-day existence. It was the Eve in both—the loving, inconsequent, tearful, smiling, erring, unphilosophic, deliciously human Eve!

"You will be enchanting always," he said, "if you steer clear of Pitt! Jealousy will not work half so much mischief with your complexion as one political argument. Read poetry and the New Testament, and have a flower garden. Don't go to the theatre! Don't go to picture galleries! Don't look at the newspapers! Don't be well informed, dear!"

"That is what Lord Wickenham says," she exclaimed. "But, of course, he doesn't call me *dear.*"

He flushed, for he had used the word unwittingly, and he was startled himself to find how much it meant—how little it might have meant. Had he not known Allegra since she was twelve years old? Had she not been in student days his pretty excuse for buying sweetmeats? Had he not always thought of her by names of endearment? His affection was so deep—so closely knit in his mind and being, that it had never known the half-ashamed self-consciousness of passion—it was, like all true love, unconscious, self-forgetful.

"You must forgive me," he said. "I forget that you are no longer a child."

Why should this delightful, ridiculous trifling be wrong? Where was the harm in these frivolous sayings? They could mean nothing. Yet, underneath them, was there not a desperate impulse to speak out—to utter things by no means frivolous, by no means trifling? Was there not a desire—as strong as all Nature—to hold Allegra a lifetime in his arms?

Warre got up from his chair and looked at his watch.

"This holiday," said he, "must satisfy me—for weeks. I am afraid it will be a long while before I see you again."

She seemed to understand and acquiesce. They had laughed aloud the comedy, and inly wept the tragedy of their fate.

"Good-bye," said he.

"Good-bye," she answered. "Will it be a cold drive home?"

"A very cold drive."

"And it must be a long while before I see you again?"

"Yes!"

"Good-bye. . . . Will there be a large fire in your study? Have you a chair you like?"

"Oh yes!"

"I suppose she sits near you when you work?"

"Who?"

"Mrs. Warre."

"You mean Anne? . . . She has a number of friends; she goes to a lot of parties. She is very . . . bright."

"Good-bye!"

This time he did not answer.

When he had gone she stole about the room, moved the ornaments on the Chinese cabinet, shook the window-curtains, and redraped them. She felt the housewife's instinct stir within her. Then she sat down on the floor, and, drawing an old letter from her bosom, murmured it backwards without once looking at the page. And she laid her head where Simon's foot had rested, and wept as little girls in the April of sorrow can weep.

CHAPTER XX

In which Warre reasons while Anne reads

WARRE, on leaving Morne House, drove to the Knightsbridge Hospital. Allegra, for the moment, was so present in his memory, that although he had wished her good-bye for what he knew must be a long, long time, he did not miss her—did not feel that the better part had fallen away irrevocably from his life. The soul is borne upon a profound emotion like a ship on a vast sea; now it seems engulfed, and now it sails serenely; it is tossed high, pitched low; sometimes it races with the wind, sometimes it seems at anchor; but underneath it there are always the rise and fall, the depths of an unfathomable ocean.

Simon was sorrowful—yes! He was used to sorrow. Self-restraint long practised will, in time, leave little to restrain. The art of dying daily is slowly mastered; but, once learnt, it becomes an instinct—an unconscious will deciding all our difficulties, solving our griefs. Now that Warre had seen Allegra, and, in their meeting, learnt all the great devotion he felt for her exacted not only from his thoughts but from his nature, he knew the uselessness of attempting to regard her as any one more sacred than a spirit, or less human than a woman. He loved her with all honour and reverence as a man should love his wife, but he could not call that surpassing affection friendship, nor could he pretend to himself that it had for its essence the false purity which makes a virtue of sexlessness. The most he could do was to kill his mortality, bury it; to look beyond his own heart and its desires; to think but of Allegra—of what, in the future before them, would be best and happiest for her. First and above all other things it was his duty to remain for ever distant from her world. He knew now that she cared for him, at least, more than a little. It was not the hour to deny, in mock modesty, this sweet and bitter truth. If they met each other often, might not this innocent preference ripen into an equally innocent but most unfortunate love? She was so young—every fair promise of earth lay written before her; she had but to accept the fulfilment of each. And Wickenham: what of him? Was he not the prince among men who deserved to win her love? Their possible marriage was the one dim brightness in Warre's sad, clouded sky. Those two, whom he held dearer than his own heart's desire, would never meet despair and desolation, or that thing so much worse than death—the knowledge that pain does not kill.

And thus it happened that, as Simon drove away from Kew, he could call Allegra beautiful and think of a committee meeting at which he was to speak in an hour's time. When he reached Knightsbridge, he looked fresher, younger, and in better spirits than his colleagues had seen him for many months. His speech was on a barren subject in connection with the management of a certain ward. To interest middle-aged and dyspeptic Science in the question of yellow as opposed to soft soap for the scrubbing of board floors requires rhetorical gifts of a high order. Simon laughed at himself and to himself when it was over and he went home. His suppressed boyishness would sometimes peep over his melancholy, just as a healthy urchin will climb an orchard wall be it never so thickly set with spears and spikes.

Anne had recovered, she said, from her headache, and, arrayed in a white silk tea-gown trimmed with chinchilla, lay on the sofa in the drawing-room, reading *Cruelle Énigme*, and coughing like Marguerite Gautier in the last act of *La Dame aux Camélias*. Mrs. Warre's desire to produce on all occasions a theatrical effect was not merely the result of her early passion for the stage and her frequent visits to the play-house. The love for the sham picturesque, for arranging tricks of light and shade and colour, for striking unusual attitudes, inventing discords, combining antagonistic colours, twisting a false knowledge of Nature into a falser presentment of life—all this is not an affectation confined to any small group of idle women, but it is the manner in art, literature, and society of modern London, modern Paris, and modern New York. Warre himself had never been able wholly to defy its fascination. Wickenham resisted its claim, but was sometimes bewildered by its glamour.

"The century is dying," he would say, "and one must humour the moribund. The thing cannot last much longer. Let us gird up our loins for a good tussle with ANNO DOMINI 1900!"

Simon now always found himself regarding Anne as though she were a mechanical puppet on show. Her clothes, her gestures, her speech, and her performance sickened his good sense, yet fixed his curiosity. Although she had utterly failed in her ambition to shine out as the great lady of this generation, she was, at least, the smartest woman in town for her little day. Her superb beauty and the splendour of her *toilettes* made her the gorgeous ornament of Private Views, First Nights, Race Courses, and the Opera; her gowns and engagements were described in *The Court Review* and all the boudoir journals; she may not have been distinguished, but she was prominent. Her dazzling prudence silenced gossip, and envy, therefore, had a richer food for spleen. Since no cardinal sin could be brought against her, suspicion, thrusting its tongue in its cheek, showed an ominous reluctance to speak words. She gave the kind no opportunity to be charitable, and the self-righteous no occasion to throw stones. The good were uneasy in her presence, and the evil, full of resentment at what they felt instinctively was not superior virtue, but a supreme gift for dissimulation. She baffled belief and hood-winked doubt. Anne had, in fact, that inhuman something which is the soul of a charlatan and the thorn in the flesh of a genius. The distinction between inhumanity and the supernatural lies in the breath—the inspiration of mortal deeds, not in the doers. There is the idea fallen from heaven, the idea risen from hell, and the idea rooted in Limbo—that sphere of unproved trespassers and unestablished saints. Any one of these three ideas will make the man or woman possessing it, remarkable; it will be the divine element in the noblest success, the terrible word in the least pitiable tragedy, or the germ of romance in the most ignominious failure. Anne Warre had made up her mind that her fate led to a high place in the world of fashion. She studied the life of Madame de Pompadour, and copied her model with the little fidelity which might be expected from an unimaginative, ill-educated woman of to-day, who would try to act the brilliant coquette and diplomatist of the eighteenth-century Versailles. She could not form an even dim conception of the creature she wished to emulate, and, dwelling on the facts rather than the circumstances of Mademoiselle Poisson's career, saw herself in power as the King's mistress, courted, feared, unquestioned, and unrestrained when there was no king, and at a period in social history when the Pompadour herself could only have gained distinction by not being the thing she was.

Warre did not know Anne's secret aspirations, but he saw her feverish discontent, her restless mind. Her face, which still kept its almost statuesque perfection of line and modelling, had now the unsatisfied, hunted look of one who is enslaved to self-advancement. Avarice had sharpened her features, steeled her eyes; long brooding on the fancied injustice of her lot had drawn her mouth into a sneer. She looked like some splendid goddess of mean evil.

As Simon entered the drawing-room, she gave him a sombre smile, and held out her hand.

"I have been wondering," she said, "why you married me, darling. If I were to die, would you grieve? If anything . . . should ever happen to me, would you feel that perhaps you had not always judged me fairly—treated me with kindness? Bourget"—she held up *Cruelle Énigme* and let two tears fall on the lovers who were pictured on the cover—" Bourget would have understood me perfectly!"

CHAPTER XXI

In which the Author speaks

WARRE had letters to write, and soon went down the stairs into his own dark study. There in that theatre of so many bitter soliloquies and so many scenes with Anne, the pregnant misery of his situation greeted him, as it were, on the threshold.

He had long suspected that Anne was involved in some miserable intrigue. Her appeal to the tribunal of Paul Bourget lifted this fear into a firm conviction. The thought of having her actions spied upon was so repugnant to his sense of honour that it did not gain a sufficient entrance to his mind to find dismissal. It would have helped him had he been able to tell his wretched story to Lord Wickenham, yet he could not repeat Anne's confessions to another. His pride, too, suffered in the humiliating knowledge that a wanton had deceived him. No man, however charitable in his judgment of a woman's weakness, but feels resentful, degraded, and ashamed when vanity lays waste the poor few sacred feet of earth he would keep consecrated and call home. No, he told himself, he could not bear pity; he could not tell his grief. And so, with the highest kind of false sentiment, he decided, like all the haughty and self-reliant in trouble, that he would bear his sorrow in silence. He overlooked, in perfect honesty and good faith, the natural intense desire to shield his own idea of his own dignity, and saw only the educated (never instinctive) wish to spare his friends a shock, which, had he allowed his experience to argue, he must have known they would have felt but slightly. Friends hear our domestic revelations with great ease, and, when they have heard all, they blame the reserve which kept them out of the secret as cowardice—not Quixotic heroism. Wrongs which are never told can never be righted.

But if Simon had been able to pierce this self-deception with clear eyes, there would still have remained, as a deterrent from any refuge in the Law, such an unfeigned compassion for the woman at stake—such an unwillingness to discover her ignominy, that, although the price of its concealment was his own lifelong captivity, he could not have found the voice to proclaim Anne's baseness.

Warre's nature was foolishly kind—sweetly,

rather than robustly chivalrous. He was not a fighter, not a soldier in the Kingdom of God, but one of those who tend the sick and wounded. He could not preach deliverance, or strike boldly at things and men corrupt. It was for him to spend his splendid energy in struggles with his own soul, and his more than womanly tenderness on beings who, for the most part, thought him clement because he lacked the courage to be severe. Warre's mental equipment was stronger than his mind. Wickenham's mind was, in those days, stronger than its equipment. Simon was not a man of one idea—of one ruling hope—one straight ambition. He had a feminine impulsiveness, and those quick-roving sympathies which can light one candle to St. Michael and the other to the Dragon. He was a dreamer of dreams, with the artist's aspirations, the ascetic's self-abnegation, the scholar's fatal hesitancy—a man who, with an almost wilfully perverse sense of what was expected of him, would, if two cups were offered for his choice, take the pewter rather than the gold, the stale beer rather than the rare wine. Such men should never have others dependent on them; they make weak fathers, foolish husbands. They are born to be loved by, and to be a killing care to, those more resolute.

CHAPTER XXII

Allegra

ALLEGRA kept her word, and remained very close to Lady Ralston all the winter. She did not see Warre again. Anne called once at Morne House, talked religion and Woman's Suffrage for fifteen minutes, and left both ladies with the feeling that, although she was beautiful and good-humoured, they would rather not discuss her charms. When they returned her visit, they were relieved to hear that she was not at home. Yet they said nothing to each other on the subject.

Lord Wickenham's friends were constant at first in their attentions and invitations to Count Vendramini's daughter, but the girl seemed to have no taste for balls or dinners, country-house parties, or the gaieties of town. It soon became the fashion to call her arrogant, *wrapt up in herself*, and cold. O these foreigners! They were very deep. She was living quietly at Kew now, because, no doubt, she thought it would be more effective to come out in the blazing noon of the London season. Clever little thing! These motherless girls were shrewd. And that old Lady Ralston. She was Scotch and canny; she never made mistakes. As for Lord Wickenham? Well, it was disappointing to see him *take up with an Italian*. A wholesome English woman was the wife for him! Of course, Allegra was half-English, but the least said about her English blood the better! Every one knew the story. Her maternal grandparents were Lord Denborough and the Duchess of A. A nice lookout for poor Wick! Why, the Duchess had ten lovers at least—O naughty lady!—and Denborough —Denborough was at once a saint, a genius, a villain, a Lovelace, a Lancelot, a Tom Jones, and a Jupiter! It was impossible to pass any judgment on the conduct of that remarkable sinner. So rumour raved and gossip clacked. Allegra heard neither.

Her time was not wasted in that apparent tomb of all work, all wit, and all ambition—Morne House, near Kew. She spent her days in parish work, and, in the evening after dinner, played Mozart and Bach till ten, when her god-mother went to bed and the gas was turned off at the meter. The parish work was arduous and exciting. Mr. Gibbs,

of St. Mary's, was Calvinistic; the Rev. Sir John
Smallpage, of Morne Chapel, followed Wyclif—till
he went too far; Mr. Wentley-Bramham was a
Moderate, a painstaking creature with nine children;
Mr. Becket Marlowe agreed with the Bishop
of Lincoln. Then there were all the curates, their
wives and families to assist, and the opposition
Congregationalists, Methodists, Baptists, Unitarians,
and Salvationists to modify and contend against.
Lady Ralston's government of these all-eloquent
worthies and their womenfolk would have taught
Prime Ministers many a useful lesson. The young
girl threw her heart into these new interests, and
tried to forget that she was working to find forgetfulness.
Yet when a night was starry, or when
snow fell and made the earth look white, or when,
at sunset, colour wove the banners of love in the sky,
or when, in the early morning, she looked out from
her window and read the promise of Summer in the
rose of a wintry dawn, tears would spring to her
eyes, and she would feel lonely—a craving for
human companionship.

But she was sincerely religious in the old
Puritanical spirit. Her Scotch nurse had taught
her a stern and simple creed which became softened
in Allegra's nature—as it did in young Milton's—
by the Pagan grace of Italy. Her God was the

Creator of a beautiful world which He loved. He did not hate it, spurn it, despise it; He had found it good when it was made, and when it became, in His sight, evil, He gave His Only Son for its redemption. In pain and sorrow, disease and death, she found but the just discipline of a True, All-wise Affection. If she sometimes seemed indifferent to praise or censure it was because she lived, not to win favours from men and women, but to serve God. She was too young not to be too independent in her ministry. Her devotion rested on that attachment to and belief in the Person of God without which faith is a mere dry mental acquiescence in useful fallacies. She did not think that to trust in the Almighty was the best mistake she could—for her own peace of life—make. It was the instinct of her soul—a fealty as intimate, inexplicable, and everlasting as the tie which sometimes binds one human being to another, and which is so far exalted above all senses and selfish sentiments that love is but its moon, and friendship but the shadow of its shadow. This sense of nearness to God and of His actual existence as the Supreme King of earth, and heaven, and hell, was the crown of the early martyrs and the sword of early Puritanism. As that knowledge grew less vivid, and scepticism—making a profession of reverence

—called this chivalric trust profane—hedging the King's Divinity about with mysteries, with insurmountable barriers of dogma and Church etiquette, so the crown was stolen and the sword became a white feather. The fear of approaching a Throne too closely and the desire to keep it inaccessible was and is ever the characteristic of those who would usurp its power—never of the faithful who would serve and protect it. Allegra, therefore, read her Bible, and, sure that her God was indeed, and in reality, God, worshipped Him as devoutly in a Protestant Chapel as at High Mass, and felt as close to Him in the common scenes of life as in the pew of an Anglican cathedral. Yet when she asked herself where she saw most piety and where she found men and women with a belief as determined as her own, it was among the poor and obscure Roman Catholics, or among English Nonconformists of the educated class. These last had often to endure ridicule and insult as the penalty of their unfashionable convictions: to be a Dissenter was to represent—in so-called polite society —all the pettiest and meanest in the human mind. Allegra had a deep respect for the clergy outside the Established Church, although Lady Ralston could only refer to them in her most generous moments as *orderly ruffians.*

The girl did not care for the meddlesome art of district visiting. She was not English, and it seemed to her democratic spirit gross insolence to pry uninvited into the homes of people, who, because they were poorer or of lower social rank than herself, were presumed to have no privacy, no pride. Lord Wickenham encouraged her feeling on this point.

"Suppose," he once said to Lady Ralston, "I were, for a change, to intrude on the rich in this neighbourhood. I should visit Lady Talbot de Lisle and say: 'Is it true, my good woman, that your husband is usually drunk, and that you have not paid your dressmaker's bill? I was greatly shocked not to see you at church last Sunday. What does this mean? Why do you allow your son to waste his time and his money on the racecourse? This is all wrong. If you want to know how to make a nourishing soup during this cold weather, put potatoe skins in the stock-pot. If you should have no stock-pot, boil vegetables in water and season them well. The French are so clever at that sort of thing! And then I should look at her as though she ought to curtsey and think me an angel. I say such things are neither kind nor virtuous; they are vulgar and disgusting. Sisters of Charity do good work because they are poor themselves ; they are not fine ladies who mistake inquisitiveness for Christian sympathy, the love of domineering for neighbourly affection, and their husband's need of votes for a wish to tend the humble. I know many poor people; I love them. I go to see them when they invite me to their homes ; they are my friends. They tell me how they suffer under this odious espionage and interference. The weak endure it because they dare not complain ; hypocrites submit to it because they hope to gain some prize for their pusillanimity ; but the strong grow sullen and desperate. There will be a revolt one day."

Lord Wickenham often came to Morne House, and Allegra enjoyed his visits till she guessed that his interest had a deeper intention than friendship. Then she became unhappy, for, while she was too modest to own in words to herself that he possibly loved her, she feared . . . she knew not what. But she opened his letters in trembling, and dreaded the pauses in their conversation. Lady Ralston, however, was nearly always present when he came, and he talked to her far more than he did to the young girl. He would bring Allegra music and picture-books and chocolate, from town ; she would play the music, look at the pictures over his shoulder, and share the chocolates with her ladyship's gasping pug-dog. Lady Ralston herself had understood Wickenham's attentions from the first, but she had also divined that her god-daughter was suffering from some secret disappointment. She could not have been so indifferent to a handsome and noble lover unless she had looked once too often on some one who seemed to her even nobler—even more handsome. There was no hope at present of Allegra's accepting any husband, and her ladyship took every precaution that Wickenham should not be tempted into a premature declaration of his hope. She trembled with apprehension when he told them that he intended to give a ball at Gifford House.

CHAPTER XXIII

Accidents and the Inevitable

LORD WICKENHAM'S ball took place on a night in April. It was a large and brilliant *function*. Royalty and aristocracy and officialdom and Mrs. Warre were present. Anne had never been so loudly admired nor more heartily detested. Wickenham — meaning to please Simon — had allowed her to figure as the inspiration of the entertainment. She had invited several enemies to witness her triumph, and a few rich friends who would know, to use her own phrase, "how to be grateful for a lift." Mr. and Mrs. Lumley-Savage were amongst the latter.

The entrance of Lady Ralston with Allegra Vendramini distracted all attention, however, from the dancing, or the supper, or the other guests. Most of the women declared that they could see nothing in the girl *to rave about*; she was so un-English. True, she knew how to dress, but she had no presence. Imagine her without that exquisite gown! How insignificant! Poor Wickenham! Captured at last by a few yards of lace and silk draped by French hands on an Italian figure! Really, it was too comic! Had he no eyes for Lady Mary's shoulders, or Lady Betty's bust, or the newest baronet's heiress's beautiful back? Mr. Stanley Breakspeare's criticism, to the effect that the future Countess of Wickenham looked like a virtuous Jan Van Beers, flew through the assembly unrivalled, till it reached the old Duke of Penhaven, who called her *une femme appétissante.*

The young girl herself was happily unconscious of the gossip she occasioned, and enjoyed—as her youth and her innocence gave her every warrant to enjoy—the music, and the flowers, and the excitement, and the waltzes.

"I wish," she said to Lord Wickenham, "that I did not feel as though it must soon strike twelve, and that everything then for me will change into rats and rags, just as it did for poor Cinderella!"

They were strolling down the picture-gallery towards one of the ante-rooms which contained a fine statue of Niobe by Bernini. His lordship frowned when Maukin-Fawkes suddenly came forward and placed himself in their way.

"I say," said he, with a pompous voice and a flurried manner, "I am sorry to interrupt you, but the most awful thing has happened. Poor old Warre had been to see a patient, and was driving here, when a cab ran into his brougham, and there's been a smash-up. They say he can't possibly live, if he isn't dead already. They have taken him to Grosvenor Street. Some one must tell Mrs. Warre. She is in there." He pointed to the ante-room, and looked narrowly into Wickenham's eyes. "She is in there with that beast, Lumley-Savage. It's very awkward!"

"Let us go to her," said Allegra; "let us go to her at once. Simon will be thinking of her—if he is not yet dead—and wondering why she does not come—wondering why he is alone. Let us go to her!"

She spoke with a composure and a tone of authority which made both men afraid. Maukin-Fawkes slunk back, but Wickenham followed her.

Anne was not in the ante-room.

Allegra covered her face with her hands. When she took them away again, she looked as though a veil of stone had been cast over her countenance.

"I want to be alone," she said to Wickenham. "I want you to leave me. I cannot speak of Simon, but I cannot speak of anything else."

Wickenham walked a little distance off to the small balcony, and the girl sat down on the pedestal at the feet of the statue of Niobe. She rested her head against that monument of imperishable grief, and her spirit seemed to grow one with it. At last, unobserved by his lordship, she stole away.

The guests were dancing. Allegra called one of the maids from the cloak-room, and, explaining that she felt unwell but did not wish to call attention to her departure, she escaped from the house by the servants' staircase.

She ordered a cab, and drove to Simon's residence in Grosvenor Street.

When she reached it, her heart regained the agony of living. She was like one who wakes in torment from the peace of a sleeping-draught. Her voice broke into tears on asking the servant for Dr. Warre. The man, she thought, seemed extraordinarily calm. She forgot that those in a doctor's service are used to seeing sorrowful and despairing visitors at every hour of the day.

She was shown into the study. Warre was sitting at his table, writing. His back was turned towards her. When he heard her name announced, he stood up, and they looked at each other as though they had each dreamed a dream which had come true.

"You!" he said.

She put out her hands and touched him.

"I thought," she whispered, "I thought you were dying. They said so . . . at the ball. That is why I came here. . . . I could not stay away."

"I am all right," he said, trying to speak lightly; "one of the horses was killed. I don't believe I have even a bruise. I am sorry you were alarmed . . . No one . . . likes to hear of a sudden accident to a friend. . . . It is good of you to have come. I cannot thank you. . . . If it had been a true report . . . this . . . this proof of your friendship would have seemed worth many deaths!"

"Oh," she cried, "if I had found you dead!"

Life and love cut the earth from their feet till they stood in that little circle where there is only space for a man and a woman and truth.

Warre took Allegra in his arms and knew her heart.

"If I had found you dead!" she repeated.

They laughed and wept, but she said no more. Then there was one vain moment when Warre kissed her face and said:

"You are mine! You are mine! Come! Let us go; let us leave all the past behind us and live our own life! I have suffered enough! Oh, come! You must never leave me again. You are mine! you are mine! let us go!"

She understood him too well to say: "What is this you are asking?"

And he understood her too well to beg her forgiveness.

It was as though those wild and foolish words had never been spoken—never been heard.

She kissed his hand and drew away.

"Is your carriage there?" he said.

"I have a cab," said Allegra. "I shall go back to Gifford Street and tell Lady Ralston where I have been."

She fastened her mantle at the throat, and wrapped her lace scarf round her head, over her face. Warre walked with her to the door, helped her into the hansom, and watched it drive towards Piccadilly.

CHAPTER XXIV

An Episode

SIMON himself went on immediately to Gifford House to reassure Lord Wickenham and Anne. But Anne was not there, and Lord Wickenham's manner was odd. Maukin-Fawkes' false news had been corrected ten minutes after he had shivered the gaiety of every one in the ball-room. The guests were all talking in little groups. Mrs. Lumley-Savage was asking all passers-by whether they had seen her husband. She was very tired, and wanted to go home. And where was her friend, Mrs. Warre? People were very polite to her—more polite than she had ever found them—and three or four great ladies called her "My dear." The Duchess of Wark offered to drive her . . . anywhere.

"But I want my husband," said the poor little woman, becoming hysterical. "Where is my husband? He knows I am not strong!"

"It is scandalous!" said Mrs. Maukin-Fawkes, in cold, prim tones. "Surely it is mistaken kindness not to tell her."

"I really think," said the Duchess to Mrs. Savage, "that it would be wiser not to wait for him."

They hustled her into her brougham—the yellow brougham lined with satin. And her lace felt heavy, and her four hundred guinea gown heavier, and her diamonds heavier yet—and her heart—so bare—so empty.

She tried to think of the children—the three little boys who made her head ache, and the little girl who cried all day from nerves.

CHAPTER XXV

Lord Wickenham's Communication to the Author

MRS. WARRE'S elopement with Mr. Lumley-Savage on the night of my ball was an event of that description which, while it excites much remark, can hardly be called a surprise. I do not think that my friend's wife was ever considered an immoral woman, or a woman who would hazard even the risk of a scandal in the cause of love, but she was, for some reason, never believed in. Savage had suddenly made an enormous and secure fortune. I feel that I do the lady no injustice when I say that his great wealth alone led her to the act, which, though in our judgment so singularly base, must have seemed to her mercenary mind most prudent. Warre's failing health had long been the secret care of those who knew and loved him. He earned a large income, but his brain was its capital, and he knew—his wife knew—we all knew, that, at the rate he worked, it could not bear the exhausting demands of another season. One or two of us felt also that there was something more than the anxiety inseparable from his profession in the boundless, ravaging ardour which consumed him. Had I not—from my knowledge of his character—believed it impossible that he could be profoundly in love, I should have said that he had either formed some disastrous attachment, or had lost—either by death or for some crueller cause—the true wife of his existence. But as he had always confided to me the secrets of his heart in matters of this nature, I certainly assumed that he was satisfied with the companionship of Mrs. Warre, and had even a genuine affection for her. She was beautiful to look at, and, in my presence, at all events, invariably showed him much devotion. I admit she may have been an accomplished actress. Before his marriage, Warre's fault was a certain insincere sentimentality, which, though it made him intimate with the poets, kept him cold—even cynical, in his relations with women. Enamoured of an imaginary excellence, he disdained the real and solid joys of life. Everything except art seemed to him grotesque. Unable to find ideal beauty, he sought ideal ugliness. He could read a ballad about love-sick lepers with pleasure, yet it shocked him to see a woman's nose grow red with weeping. I speak now of his bachelor days. He altered. I discouraged his engagement with Miss Delaware, but when I observed them together after their marriage, I often found myself wondering whether it had not proved, on the whole, a successful experiment—seeing that neither of them were persons of deep feeling. I am telling you all this to show you how men may be deceived in appearances, and how much we may be mistaken in our estimate even of those we know most intimately.

Warre bore his wife's infidelity with an absence of resentment which, I must confess, struck me at first as pusillanimous. He refused to divorce her, and refused to discuss her conduct. He continued his life, unmoved, with a dogged and stubborn persistence, which placed him beyond the range of criticism, because it seemed outside the pale of what was human, of what was common, or even uncommon, in men's experience. The soul and the manhood within him were dead. I say it now with bitter self-reproach, but, at that period, I lost all interest in him. He repelled me. I could not understand him. He made it clear, I thought, that he did not wish to be understood; he asked nothing, so it seemed, but to be let alone. Mrs.

Warre and Savage went on a yachting cruise with a party of congenial friends around the world. Simon was still a young man, and we all laboured to convince him, that, if he would but divorce his wife, he could marry again. He made his life so much harder, so much more difficult than it need have been. The law was made to protect us from ourselves and from each other; to redress grievances, to preserve peace and equity and happiness It is surely our own fault if we suffer an injustice for which both the Church and the State offer us a remedy. But he would listen with hopeless eyes and unheeding ears to all I said. Once he reminded me that there was no child in the question. If there had been a child, he would have felt it his duty to protect it from such a mother; he would have taken steps . . . he would have fought a duel to the death, but . . . He never finished the sentence.

At last, after a blank and dreary interval of time, he told me that he had undertaken the management of a colonial hospital at a place which I knew well he hated, and in a climate which he knew, to a certainty, would painfully kill him. Then he spoke out.

"Wick," said he, "I know your kindness, and if I had a living heart I would thank you for it.

Now I am going away, I feel I can tell you something which, had I stayed in England, must have ever remained a secret. I loved Allegra. I never loved Anne at all."

This revelation took away my breath. I could make no answer. I had known ever since the night when the false report came of his accident that Allegra cared—in no merely childish measure—for him. The knowledge was a grief to me, for it was the death-warrant of my own foolish hope. She was not one to have two loves in her life. And—even though I might have been the gainer had she been less faithful—I could not have wished her to be otherwise.

"I loved Allegra," he repeated. "I love her always. But if I were to get my freedom—if she were an older woman—if she had lived and suffered and known disappointment, and worked folly, and suffered remorse, I should not even then be justified in asking her to share my life. I have nothing now but memories I may not speak of, self-doubts I dare not own, a habit of silence which I shall never shake off. I have seen the vision of sin and corruption; my eyes are seared with it. I am a man broken in health and heart; the hand of death is upon me. I can never more feel either love or sorrow. I am speaking truth, Wick. Nothing can ever hurt me again."

I felt that he was right. My poor friend had so completely and so cruelly severed himself from every emotion in life, that there was already the something forbidding, unapproachable, awful about him, which we recognise in the laid-out body, even of one who was most dear and familiar to us when living.

He left England that night. When he said good-bye to me, I knew that I saw him for the last time on earth. His face was already transparent, and the glory of the incorruptible shone through. He was not yet so dead but that he looked wistful as the train steamed from the platform. We waved handkerchiefs; his soon became a speck in the distance—and finally, nothing.

And now I must speak briefly. Allegra rarely mentioned Warre's name to me; laughing and chatting of gaieties, she pined away. I watched the change in her countenance week by week; they took her to the south of France. I went there, too; she said I amused her. I never once saw her look sad, nor did I ever hear her complain at her illness. Indeed, she appeared unconscious of it, and seemed to think that she was at Cannes because her father suffered from gout. When, at length, our distress at her condition betrayed itself, she used to write me little notes in pencil to assure me that although her voice was weak, she had a great deal to say. These letters were hard to read; I have six of them. I fancy that the word *Simon* occurs in the last. One evening, when I thought that the end was near, I received word of his ship's safe arrival in Africa, and of his death on board the vessel. He died in his sleep, and they buried him at sea. The man who sent the news wrote like a lawyer, and I was grateful for his curtness. I could not have borne, at that moment, very kind or very graphic words.

I, who knew Allegra's secret, feared that this sorrow would do the worst. I took counsel with the Count and Lady Ralston, and we resolved to withhold the sad tidings. But, as I was sitting by her side the following day, pretending to read while she pretended to sleep, she startled me by saying in a whisper:

"Do you know, I have long had a feeling that Simon is dead. I am not so lonely as I used to be. I can almost believe that he is with me." And she wept.

"And if he should be dead?" I asked.

For a moment she seemed to regain all her sweet health and vigour:

"I should get well," she answered, "for then I should know that he was at rest—that he was happy."

With women all things are possible. I cannot explain Allegra's strangeness, but whatever she said or did always seemed right and natural. Such was her peculiar force of character. I forgot to marvel at the mystery before me, and told her quietly that her foreboding was true. Simon was dead. They had buried him at sea. Tears streamed down her cheeks while she listened; she held out her hands and clasped—what looked to me—the air.

"At last," she said, "at last, he is free. He can never be sorrowful again. Oh, my very dearest! I do not call you back!"

Her religious faith was the purest and most beautiful I have ever known or conceived of. Her belief in God and the angels and the other world gave confidence and courage even to those whose lives were spent in questions, and who could hope to find no answer to them all in death. If I should say how dear I held even the privilege of seeing her, it might sound extravagant. Many weeks passed before she became so much as convalescent, but she lived, and still lives. I always fear that there is something not unlike profanity in daring to love her with a man's love. I try to feel it even when I am most desolate—even when I look about me and see other men who have wives and children to love and by whom they are loved. I am no celibate by instinct; I do not care much for unmarried people, or for people who have not, at all events, a love of family life—an idea of home well knit in their bones and tissue.

But so many of us, like Warre, have noble ideals, and then, because we cannot see them realised immediately, we accept, in a moment of petulance, the lesser thing. There is a king's daughter for each one of us; let us wed her or none other. And so with every aim and hope in life. We should do nothing—we should say nothing—we should content ourselves with nothing which seems to fall below the highest we can think of. Then, if we should find disappointment, or should we be deceived, we can at least say—We took thee, best and dearest, for the best thou shouldst have been. But to be fooled, knowing well that we had chosen to be fooled—chosen the false in mere impatience with our quest of the true—that is what really degrades us—really causes despair.

Warre took the lesser thing. That is the sum of his folly. I loved him well; his disposition had a divine sweetness. But he was not a man to make men strong or to lead a woman's will. I trust I say this without jealousy. But I cannot be sure. For it is true that I envy him, although his body is one with the sands of the sea, and his grief was more than he could tell, and his life, in men's judgment, a failure.

CHAPTER XXVI.

The Last.

THE reader who has followed Warre's story to its close will find no cause for wonder in the discovery that even Lord Wickenham never completely grasped his character or his motives. Simon never spoke out, and he was therefore never understood. And his lordship, although a gentleman to whose honour, generosity, and unselfishness I have never found a parallel, was jealous of his dead rival. He knew it, deplored it, struggled right valiantly against it, but the passion remained. Yet, if he had ever conquered this natural weakness, I think I should not have liked him half so well. Allegra herself once confessed to me that she never felt such affection for him as when he tried to speak with fairness—and could not—of poor Warre. She was a true woman.

Lumley-Savage lived but ten months with Anne, for he caught typhoid fever and died, leaving his vast fortune to his wife and children. Mrs. Warre has gone on the stage, and, when I last heard of her, she was playing the part of *Lady Jane Grey* in a tragedy, and living under the protection of a Worshipful Cheesemonger. She wears a mourning ring for Simon, and cries bitterly when his name is mentioned.

"My God!" she invariably says, "he was a good man. And I shall never love any one else—never, never, never love any one else!"

And this depresses the Worshipful Cheesemonger.

As I write these last words, a letter reaches me from Allegra.

"My dear friend," she says. "Wick and I are of course deeply interested to hear of this romance you are weaving about gods and mortals. We want you, however, to write a biography of Simon Warre. Let it be a truthful history. Do not tell his story the way it did not happen. You knew him as none of us knew him. But I loved him the best. I did—indeed, I did!

"Yours ever affectionately,

"ALLEGRA WICKENHAM."

I believe that she loved him the best—that she

loves him the best still. And the words Lord Wickenham wrote me two years ago would be his words to-day:

"I envy him, although his body is one with the sands of the sea, and his grief was more than he could tell, and his life, in men's judgment, a failure."

THE END.

Printed by Hazell, Watson, & Viney, Ld., London and Aylesbury.

www.ingramcontent.com/pod-product-compliance
Lightning Source LLC
Chambersburg PA
CBHW031332230426
43670CB00006B/327